WHY NOT YOU?

How to Become an EMPOWERED Woman

DR. VAL MARGARIT

Why Not YOU

Copyright © 2017 by Dr. Val Margarit

Publisher:
Val Margarit Consulting Services
val@valmargarit.com

Publishing consultant:
Professional Woman Publishing, LLC
www.pwnbooks.com

ISBN: 978-0-578-19472-1

Contents

Foreword

When Val called me four weeks ago to tell me she was writing this book, she asked me if I would write its foreword. "Absolutely NOT", I answered. "Writing a foreword is for celebrities or published authors, neither of which is my case." I paused for effect. "So anyway, what's this book about?" I asked, hoping for an obscure academic topic that would automatically remove me from being a foreword-writer candidate. "Well, it's about empowerment, you know, teaching women how to be strong and successful." I wriggled in my chair, looking for an easy way out. "Sounds awesome and pretty complicated. Surely you have more qualified friends, you know, younger, more successful, more tuned into this new age than I am…" Val kept insisting that I was her only choice and my suspicion grew that I was probably the only one to take her phone call that morning! When I voiced my thoughts about previous calls she probably had made, she was indignant and insistent. "You are my first and only choice, and it means the world to me to have you, my *first* mentor, write the foreword to my first book!" More compliments followed, and soon I was boxed into a corner with no way out. "Okay then, at least send me a draft of the book, so I know what I will be "forewording"! This was said in the futile hope that she wouldn't have a draft copy to send me, or it would get lost in the cloud (I've always been suspicious of something I have never seen that is somehow storing all my special documents). The thought that, worse yet, the book would turn out to be very helpful and practical advice needed by thousands of women struggling to achieve their dreams and I would be compelled to write the foreword after all. Obviously, it turned out to be the latter. Therefore, here is my reluctant attempt.

Val's book starts off with an introduction to the fourteen years she spent growing up in a small, rural village in Romania. It was a world that most of her readers would have difficulty imagining: living in a house with electricity but no indoor plumbing (yes, that means no daily shower or a sit-down flush toilet), two black and white TV channels that produce nothing but static, endless farming chores like pulling weeds and loading produce into a truck, walking two miles one way to school (sometimes in deep snow) and worst of all, NO CELL PHONE!

And there was worse to come: Val had to find a job before she could start her high school education! Let's face it, most of us would have given in to deep depression and/or vodka only halfway through the story. Yet Val not only escaped her childhood with a deep desire to make her parents proud, but her early experiences ignited her fierce ambition to achieve a better life no matter what the odds.

This is the background of the woman whom I hired as a shipping clerk about a year after she arrived in the U.S.A. Having met my husband when he was a political refugee from Bulgaria (you know, that Eastern European country that produced all the killers in the James Bond movies), I had some ideas about how to help Val adjust to this new world, and she took all my suggestions to heart (particularly the one about Bulgarian boyfriends…).

It was soon obvious that Val would have absolutely no problems in this country. She signed up for free classes to improve her English, purchased a car and was making secret plans to take over my job when she was (luckily) diverted by her acceptance into Miami Dade College. Soon she was on her way to getting an Associate's Degree while supporting herself working full time. I was amazed at her energy and adaptability and gave her credit for the level of intense focus with which she pursued her goals. I have never seen anyone as committed and focused as she was. I followed her progress with fascination, even visiting one of the "apartments" she could afford, a one-room "cave" with books stacked nearly to the ceiling and no obvious sleeping area or indoor plumbing (it felt like home, so it must have reminded her of Romania).

Now that I have read Val's book on empowerment, I recognize the decisions she made to choose her friends and mentors carefully and to remove herself from any negative environments. Val believed that her environment affected her choices and her future and as such, she thoughtfully detached herself from any negative people and environments. She was true to herself and to her priorities. As Gloria Steinem said, "The truth will set you free, but first it will piss you off!"

As Val continued her whirlwind academic career, she decided that it was important and necessary to run a marathon, and not just any marathon, but the New York City Marathon! I tried to explain to Val that it would be a long, grueling experience that would tear her heart out and offer no prize money at the finish line. Val believed she needed the challenge to strengthen her mental ability, as she believed that the mind controls the body and not the other way around. Indeed, the marathon training prepared her for another "marathon" later on, the completion of a doctoral degree program. Val went about her business in the usual methodical way, setting up a training schedule and running every day while tracking and measuring her progress on a whiteboard. And she has used the same approach with every goal she has decided to achieve. She lives with intention and purpose. Her enthusiasm is contagious.

Now let's turn to the topic at hand, understanding how important it is for women to be empowered in all areas of their lives. Let's start with politics (which is on everyone's mind right now). Marching on Washington was great theater and produced a great deal of media attention, but it won't change the laws of the land unless we, as empowered women, continue to act on our beliefs and values. Val is committed to improving the political environment for women. Her dedication to positive change is strong. She lives it, breathes it, and teaches it. She was recently elected President of her Home Association Board. Who knows what her next political step will be. Perhaps she will run for a public office, in which, I believe, she will be terrific.

Professional life is another area where women continue to seek empowerment. The television show, *Mad Men,* was a reminder of how laughably bad things were just a generation ago. Yes, there has been some progress, but it is still an uphill battle. With more empowered women in the work force, there could be a new era of equality in opportunity. Val was always the perfect example of an empowered woman in the business world. Even twenty years ago when she had very little business experience and her English was still shaky, Val was asked by my husband, the general manager, how she saw her future in our company. Her answer was: "I want to sit in your chair." He knew then she would go far professionally because she was not afraid to speak up for herself and her values. She was already planning her successful future.

As for financial empowerment, unfortunately, too many women face pay inequality in the workplace. Women still earn significantly less than men for equal work and are less likely to be considered for high paying jobs and promotions. Women also need to become more equal partners at home. I have seen firsthand the classic story of a husband dying suddenly, leaving his wife with little or nothing, because he had not properly managed the family finances and she had not been involved in their financial decisions. Empowered women who take control of their finances become more independent and confident of their future. Val is committed to teaching women how to become financially empowered as she did.

Physical fitness is an important part of Val's recipe for empowerment. As she explains in the book, staying in shape and taking care of her health is the best way for an empowered woman to live. Feeling good enables her to achieve her goals.

Though reluctant at first, I have enjoyed writing this foreword, because it made me reflect on how important empowerment is in a woman's life. The truth is that whoever reads this book will be inspired to change and to help other women change.

Help one another. Empower one another. What a world this will be when we empowered women reach all our goals! We deserve it and the world will be better for it!

Sharon K. Andonov

Acknowledgments

Thank you to my family, who taught me to follow my dreams and to work as long as it takes to achieve my goals. You instilled in me the confidence that I could do anything I put my mind to and for believing in me that as a 16 years old teenager, I was ready to leave the house in pursuit of a better life. Thank you for raising me to believe I could become whatever I wanted to become as long as I work hard for it. Thank you for being the best parents I could ever have. I miss you both terribly.

Thank you to my first mentors, Sharon and Dimitri, who believed in me when I was barely speaking English and had nothing but BIG dreams. Your constant support, guidance and love have made all the difference in my life and I will be forever grateful.

Thank you to every teacher and coach I had throughout my life. Thank you for the inspiration, motivation and belief that I was capable to achieve anything I wanted as long as I persisted and didn't give up.

Thank you to all the women reading this book. My hope is that it will inspire you to change your life. I look forward to meeting you one day.

Thank you to all my friends and supporters for always being there for me and for inspiring me every step of the way.

I feel so lucky to be surrounded by all of you.

For more information on programs and services, please visit *www.valmargarit.com*

Introduction

Are you living up to your full potential? Are there aspects of your life that you wish you could improve? If you are tired of living your life by the standards of others, it is time to make the changes necessary to live the life you deserve. I have yet to meet one woman from the many I have worked with over the years that believes she is using her full potential. You must decide to start living your life and bring purpose to it by finding out what matters most to you.

You need to become self-empowered. Self-empowerment[1] calls for a self-evaluation of your true values and aspirations. What do you want to achieve today, next week, next year, five years from now? What do you value and do you live in harmony with those values? Are you doing anything today that will ensure a better tomorrow? What do you want out of life? What is your passion? You need to be able to answer all of these questions in a way that resonates with who you truly are. If you are not happy with your life today, and you don't take steps to change it, how can anything be different in the future? Are you ready to take action and decide "enough is enough" and that today you will commit to doing whatever it takes to change your life and become self–empowered?

If you're reading this book, chances are you said 'yes' and are ready to start your journey to self-empowerment. Never before has it been as possible as it is today to attain a successful, purpose-driven life. Indeed, the Internet has revolutionized the way we live our lives and the possibilities are everywhere.

For example, you can start an online business today, as I did, sign up for online courses to learn new skills, as I did, or pursue a college degree as I did. Moreover, you can join a support group, network with other like-minded people, and even invite your friends and family along for support and accountability. It is possible today more than at any other time in our history to pursue your dreams and live the life you deserve. Make your life count. You owe it to yourself.

Self-empowerment means to be in control of every area of your life: health, career, finances, spiritual, political, and emotional. Only then will you be empowered and happy.

It is a common saying that money will not buy happiness, and I think that is true. However, we cannot be happy if we do not have financial freedom. Likewise, we cannot be happy if we are not healthy and respectful of our bodies. Nor can we be happy if our focus is only on ourselves with little regard for those less fortunate who may need our help. The same goes for our career where we often accept what is convenient but not meaningful and politics where laws that affects our livelihood are often decided by men.

Each of us has a powerful mind. We are entitled to meaningful work, excellent health, financial independence, political representation and happy relationships. You have untapped talent and extraordinary ability within you, and once you believe that, you will be able to achieve everything you want in life. Once you change your thinking and circumstances, your life will change forever.

The primary goal of this book is to teach you how to live your life in alignment with your values. You will learn the skills, principles, and systems you need to empower yourself. You will come to appreciate the power of your thinking and how to change negative into positive thoughts. You will learn how to communicate and advocate for what you believe in, how to manage your finances, as well as how to use S.M.A.R.T. goals settings to achieve any goal. Your health is paramount to your happiness, and I will teach you the importance of caring for yourself and adopting a healthy lifestyle. In the end, you will know how to take care of your mind, body, and soul, all of which are imperative to your overall success and happiness.

Don't be scared or afraid. There is nothing to fear since you already know your life is your own to live the best way you can. No one is responsible for your success but yourself, and waiting around for someone to save you is not an option. You already have within you everything you need to change your life. Yes, you will make mistakes. That is part of the learning process but you will keep moving forward. By doing so, you will become more courageous, confident, resilient, and able to take on even bigger challenges in your journey toward self-empowerment. I guarantee you that.

I have learned that self-empowerment is a state of mind. You have to believe and decide for yourself that you deserve to be successful and happy and that you will live your life with purpose and intention. You cannot control or change events or people, but you can change how you react to what happens to you. You can change yourself and become the person you wish to be.

Are you ready to begin this journey with me? Get ready, my friend. This is the beginning of a transformative journey, and I will be by your side every step of the way.

Let's begin. We cannot afford to wait any longer; the clock is ticking.

My Story

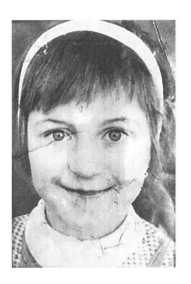

To know me you need to know where I come from.

I come from a small village in Romania[2] where the population is only 400. It's far out of the way of any city and for the longest time, I used to joke that my village was not even on the map. It is on the map, of course, located about 103 km or 64 miles from Romania's capital, Bucharest, and about 74 km or 46 miles from Braila, the district capital and my birthplace.

My two sisters, Steluta, eight years older and Georgica, six years older, had already left home for school by the time I was old enough for us to play or study together. Therefore, I grew up as an only child, helping my parents with the farm, taking care of animals and planting tobacco and corn in the fields. It was hard work for a child but I was expected to work alongside my parents after school hours and during vacations. Farm life was not easy. I grew up without indoor plumbing, with floors and ceilings of hard clay, and a two-channel black and white TV that did not work most of the time. I never owned or played with a doll as a child, which was common in my village. Instead, I used stones, beans, sand, and wood as my toys since they were all that was on hand. I had to create my playground with the things available around me. We were mostly self-sufficient, producing our own food, and raising our own livestock. We grew tomatoes, grapes, potatoes, corn, and other vegetables in the gardens and raised pigs, chickens, and cows.

I watched my parents work so hard every day, from dawn to dusk and that is not what I wanted for my future. My father, Dobre, only had an 8th grade education. My mother, Maria, never attended school and only learned to read and write much later in life. My mother told me she did not go to school because she had no shoes. There was no money left for her after her parents had bought shoes for her older sisters. When I heard my mother's story, I was so shocked and upset and I determined this would never happen to me. It was my mother's lack of education that fueled my passion and need for change. I realized how hard life had been for my mother. For most of her life she, who could neither read nor write, but had to rely on her husband and others for help and severely limited her experience of the world. This awareness deeply affected me in my young life. Although not yet familiar with the term "self-empowerment," I knew I had to get an education for myself and for the women and girls who were not able to realize their full potential because they lacked the opportunity to attend school. I knew that education was the key to freedom.

There was only one school in my village for grades one through eight. When it was time for me to attend ninth grade, I had to commute to the nearby village of Ciocile[3] with a much larger population of 3000. There was no school bus so we walked about two miles each way weighed down by a backpack full of books. When I finished 10th grade, I was eager to continue my education, even though that meant I would have to move away from home. Luckily, this was easier because I had my parents' full support. I wanted a better life than they had and they supported my dream.

Although my parents did not have a formal education, they taught me the value of hard work, perseverance, and to never give up on my dreams. They did not want my gender or my geographical location to decide my future. They wanted me to decide my own future based on my own abilities. That mindset allowed me to believe that I could achieve anything as long as I never gave up. We will discuss more about the importance of mindsets later in the book.

Despite the circumstances of my upbringing, I had a happy childhood and loving and caring parents. My parents were compassionate and loving, even while they had high expectations and strict rules. Our way of life may have brought these characteristics out in my parents, but the way my parents raised me certainly contributed to the adult I became. My parents expected me to do well in school, be proud of myself, complete my household chores, respect everyone, work hard, never complain, and never give up on achieving my dreams. They raised me to believe that I was as smart as I was beautiful and that if I wanted something in life, I would have to work hard to get it. And that's what I did: after finishing the tenth grade, I left my family to continue my education and find a job. I was ready to fly, to be independent and face my life head on.

A high school friend had already left her village and had found a job 40 km away in a small town in a clothing factory, sewing garments. My determination to leave farm life behind to continue my education meant that any job was better than farming. Therefore, armed with a strong work ethic and an aggressive mindset, I was ready to enjoy my independence, completely unaware what the job was about or that the job shift started at 5:00 am.

On My Own For The First Time

I was two months shy of my sixteenth birthday when I left home for the first time.

My dad gladly embarked on this new journey with me as we traveled 40 km together to the town of Lehliu. There was a position open at the same factory where my friend worked, so we headed there to apply for the job only to find out that I had to be sixteen to get a job legally. The delay was painful for me, focused as I was on starting my new independent life. It was horribly frustrating to go back home for two excruciatingly long months. Looking back on this time, I realize now that this was my first important lesson: by not giving up, I experienced first-hand that persistence is necessary to achieve any goal, exactly what my parents had repeated to me day after day while growing up: Do the best you can with every opportunity you have, and be persistent all the way to the end. Two months later, I showed up at the factory, completed the required documents, found a room to share with three other girls and settled in.

I had never sewed or touched a sewing machine, but my goal was not to become a seamstress. I had bigger and higher goals for myself, and learning to sew was a stepping-stone to achieving them. That approach has helped me throughout life, and I quickly learned never to complain or be afraid of the unknown or hard work. I began a new chapter in my life, working in a clothing factory during the morning shift, from 5:00 am to 2:00 pm. It was a giant step forward to a better life, but also a reminder of how far I still had to go. I never enjoyed working at the factory (as you can see in the photo) but I did what I had to do.

Easy to spot me – the last, not too happy

Once I was confident in my job, I enrolled in night classes to complete my last two years of high school. It was quite an ordeal, and looking back, I wonder now how in the world I did it. Just as I learned about persistence in those miserable two months at home waiting to start a job, now I was learning that although I was doing what I had planned to do, it was not fun. But it was necessary! After all, success is not just about what you do but who you become.

Two years later, I graduated with my high school diploma, and it was time for me to move on to something better than getting up at 5:00 in the morning and working in a factory! Please, I had left farming behind, and now it was time to leave the factory behind and put my high school degree to work. My move to Bucharest, the capital of Romania, was overwhelming for a young high school graduate from a tiny farming village but a necessary step I knew I had to take, knowing that this new exciting environment would challenge, inspire and motivate me for even bigger challenges. The next six years were filled with new experiences, and new people and I learned that our environment affects how we think, feel and ultimately behave. Now I was ready to move yet again.

Pursuing A Dream

It was December 14, 1996, when I arrived at Miami International Airport, the day I hoped my life would change forever. I knew that if I made it to America, I would be able to pursue my dreams and live the life I always wanted. I remember growing up watching American movies such as *Dallas*[4], and *Rich Man, Poor Man*[5] and thinking how amazing it would be to live in America, pursuing the American Dream. I dreamed of becoming like Rudy in the movie *Rich Man, Poor Man*, a well-educated and ambitious entrepreneur. Ready to make my American dream a reality, I believed that nothing and no one would stop me. After all, I had the mindset of success; always focus on making progress, learn from setbacks, always challenging myself and believing that I deserved the best for myself and everyone around me.

Before I even landed at Miami International Airport, I was planning my job search strategy. I only had a few hundred dollars to my name, and I needed to find a source of income as soon as possible. Since I did not have a car, I had to look for a job within walking distance from my apartment. About half a mile from my apartment was Alton Road, a very popular street full of restaurants, cafes, and exclusive shops. I walked into a busy beachwear store to apply for a job, met the owner and asked to interview for a sales associate position. To my surprise, he needed to hire someone right away and after a brief interview; I was asked when I could start. So naturally, I said, "NOW" and started to work. The first thing I did at the end of the day was to call my parents: "Hello, Mom, Dad, you won't believe what just happened. I got a job! Yes, two days in America and I just got hired".

It was an unbelievable feeling and confidence booster. I thanked my parents for everything they had done for me and for the values they had instilled in me, values that had guided me in both good and bad times to do the right thing and never settle for less than what I deserved. Like any other teenager, I thought my parents were too strict and that they had asked too much of me. As I learned later however, they were only preparing me for the real world. To them, it was important for me to understand that the real world was nothing like home. Before hanging up the phone, I thanked my parents, told them how much I loved and missed them.

Time For a New Job

I was at my first job as a retail sales associate for about a year when I decided it was time to move on to better things. After a year in retail sales in Miami Beach, FL, I knew it was time to move to a more challenging and rewarding job. I saw a notice for a job as a front desk receptionist at a nearby tourist hotel posted on a local bulletin board. I researched the type of guests the hotel catered to and visualized myself on the job, charming the arriving guests and learning all about them and their cultures. I believed I could get the job, borrowed a nice suit from a friend, and, no surprise, I was hired.

I learned early in life that having dreams and goals without a plan of action to achieve them does not mean anything. Right? Think about it. Every person has dreams and goals, but not everyone pursues them, and even fewer people achieve them. Why? There are many reasons but I believe the most prominent are a lack of belief in oneself, confidence, persistence, support, and the understanding that failure is part of success, that it takes discipline and a tolerance for hard work.

All of these topics will be discussed later in the book, with suggestions on how to create an effective strategy for the pursuit and achievement of your goals. It is possible. So why not take advantage and become the person you always wanted to be? Do not worry; I will show you how to change your life for the better and achieve anything you want. You have to believe that you deserve it and be willing to change to attract the things you want in your life.

> *"I didn't get there by wishing for it or hoping for it, but by working for it."*
>
> —Estee Lauder

Coaching Moment

Regardless of where you are in life, it is never too late to change it for the better. Change begins with you. Think about it – what do you have to lose? Everything if you do not take risks and give yourself the opportunity to live an amazing life. Your life will only get better the more you know yourself and the more chances you take. There is no better time to begin planning for a better life than NOW. If you are not satisfied with your current job, then come up with a plan and do something about it. This book will help you with that.

I made a plan to get out of my tiny village and away from the farm but I didn't stop there. I dreamed of educating myself and pursuing my passion and dreams. I never wanted to be average. The world is full of average people. You and I can do better. Once you have identified your dreams and ambitions, never give up on them. Put yourself first and work hard for your happiness; you deserve it!

The Power of Association

"Alone we can do so little; together we can do so much."

—Helen Keller

One of my favorite expressions and one you've probably heard is that you are the average of the five people you spend the most time with, for better or worse. Another favorite expression of mine is, show me who your friends are, and I will tell your future. Take a moment and think about these quotes. Who are the five people in your life that you spend the most time with? What do you have in common with them? Do they motivate and inspire you to become better?

When I first arrived in Miami, I didn't have five people to spend time with. I definitely didn't have people supportive of my big dreams and goals. However, once I started my job as a front desk receptionist, I loved it as I was meeting new people from all over the world, learning new skills, and improving myself in every area of my life. I lived in a beautiful city and had so many opportunities but I realized that I needed some support and guidance to make sense of this new life. I decided to reach out and invest my time and energy in people who would support my efforts to achieve my goals, who would push me to become better in every way and who would believe in me, especially in uncertain times. I wanted smart, strong and wise friends so I could become like them. That is exactly what I saw in Dimitri and Sharon as they walked up the front desk to check in. "Hello," I said in a cheerful voice, "Welcome to Kenmore Hotel, my name is Val, and I am here to help you."

The couple was pleasantly surprised by my professionalism and friendly personality and asked me where I was from. I told them I was from Romania. I learned that Dimitri, the husband, was a native of Bulgaria and Sharon, his wife, was American born. They met and lived overseas before moving back to the United States and settling in Milwaukee, where they raised a family and lived for twenty years. Once their children went off to college, they decided it was time to leave Milwaukee for South Beach. Not a bad choice, I thought.

Dimitri and Sharon were house hunting in Miami Beach and stayed at the hotel where I worked. With every visit, I learned more and more about them and found out that we had much in common. I learned that they both were educated and accomplished and had encountered many setbacks in their professional careers. However, they never gave up on their dream to pursue higher education degrees and to own their own business one day, despite the many challenges presented along the way.

Hearing their personal story of triumphs and downfalls was like a light bulb going on over my head. I thought that if Dimitri, whose story was very similar to mine in many aspects, could do it, then so could I.

Our conversations at the hotel started our friendship: I would eagerly ask questions about how to make it in America, and they would welcome my curiosity with inspiring but honest answers. We had a mutual respect for one another, and they were in turn impressed with my dedication and commitment to succeed in my new country. Over their many visits to Miami Beach, we grew to know each other well and one day they asked if I would join them for dinner. My answer was a decisive YES. I was so excited, believing that my life was about to change again and I was ready for a bigger challenge.

We had a great time over dinner getting to know each other, sharing stories and dreams and before I knew it, the evening concluded with an offer. Yes, a job opportunity. I guess I must have made a good impression! I was so excited and in awe that I immediately said YES. What was there to think about? I would have worked for them for free just to have the opportunity to learn from them.

I showed up at my new job ready for the new challenge, which lasted for the next two years: two years of incredible, personal and professional development. Sharon and Dimitri became my mentors, my "adopted parents," my employers, teachers, and friends. They introduced me to different educational resources, and advised on proper communication and social behavior. They inspired and motivated me to be courageous and to pursue my goals, exactly as my parents had taught me. Now I had direction. I had someone in my corner believing in me and supporting my aspirations. I knew that if I worked hard, listened closely, took their advice, evaluated and reassessed my progress, I would achieve my goals as they had done. I looked up to them because they were the success story that I wanted for myself.

"I believe people are in our lives for a reason.
We're here to learn from each other."

—GILLIAN ANDERSON

At the time, my main aspiration was higher education. Education was important to me from an early age, and I always wanted to learn as much as I could. First, it was a way to escape the harsh village life, but then I realized that knowledge is power and I could use it to improve every area of my life and to help others along the way. So, with my mentors' help, I decided it was time for my next challenge, going to college. I knew that if I wanted to become empowered, in control of my life and have a platform to express and share my ideas to help others achieve their own goals, then I needed an education. I was excited, nervous, and anxious but most of all, I was grateful to have the opportunity to go to college and earn a college degree. I would be the first in my family to achieve such a thing. After all, I was in the United States where opportunities were everywhere for those of us who were willing to work hard and get things done. I saw challenges as opportunities to learn and grow. Indeed, I was raised to not take anything for granted or complain but instead to find solutions and create the life I wanted to have. *To live my life by design not by chance.*

Sharon and Dimitri have been my mentors for 20 years now. Without their insights, support, and guidance my personal success would have taken a longer time. I recognized the opportunity to join their circle and learn everything they knew about overcoming challenges and achieving success in a new country. Yes, I was hungry to learn, evolve, and succeed and I knew that mentorship was the way to go. They have been perfect mentors because, like me, they never stopped pursuing and achieving their own goals despite challenges and setbacks along the way. I am fortunate to have them in my life today and to know that I could pick up the phone at any time and ask for advice.

Soon I added more people of value to my circle of influence, such as Dr. Joan Morris, who has been my mentor since my third year in college studying sociology and that was about fifteen years ago. As soon as Dr. Morris walked into my sociology class at the University of Central Florida, I knew that I had to ask her to become my mentor because her story in many aspects was similar to mine. She went to school later in life, finished her doctoral degree at 39 years old, and had to overcome many challenges along the way, such as raising a child. Nothing had stopped her from achieving her goals; she became my third perfect mentor. Without hesitation, she was more than willing to share her experience and expertise with me. I am grateful to have her in my life still today. This is how I added value to my life: by always seeking out people who were already successful in life doing the things I wanted to do. Recall that you are the average of the five people you spend most of your time with, so choose wisely.

Build Your Team of Winners

"A mentor is someone who allows
you to see the hope inside yourself"

—OPRAH WINFREY

To create a winning team that will help you achieve your own success, you need to have a strategy and ask yourself a few questions.

1   Whom do you admire and trust?

Take account of the people in your life that you admire and pick their brains about their education, aspirations, and goals and how they achieve them. Find out if they are supportive of your own goals. What if they are not? Will you be ready to cut them loose? We cannot replace our family, but when it comes to the people we spend time with, we need to be careful. The company we keep will influence how we feel and who we become, so always be surrounded by like-minded individuals. If those people are not helping you become better, smarter and wiser, then it is time to look for new friends who will help you achieve your dreams.

2   Do you know of someone who has already achieved what you want to achieve?

Look them up online, call their office, or send an email asking to meet for coffee and pick their brain. Learn as much as you can about them before the meeting and prepare a set of questions to ask. Perception is reality so make sure you make a great first impression. Be prepared, polite, friendly and on time. Be persistent and do not give up finding mentors that will be willing to help you. Persistence pays off. Always. Trust me.

3   Are you ready for a mentor?

The lessons you will learn from your mentors are priceless. What are you going to do with the newfound knowledge? Will you be ready to put it into action? It is only then that knowledge becomes useful. Use this information to change your life and become empowered.

4   Do you need to improve your networking skills?

Whether you love to network or not, in today's world, networking is a necessity. Plenty of research[6] shows the value of networking. It leads to more business opportunities, faster advancement, greater status, better quality of life and job satisfaction. It is up to you to take the plunge and look up networking groups for the areas you need to improve your skills set.

I always seek out different networking groups, as I know that I have much to learn and much to share, which makes it a win-win experience. I take a positive attitude and curiosity to learn about other people and to expand my knowledge. I usually leave my network meetings inspired and motivated to try new things or implement a new way of doing business. Networking is powerful, and it will empower you. It will change your life.

We are all in this together. Together we are stronger than apart. So, why not help each other become our best selves? Surround yourself with positive people who care for, support you, and always strive for everyone to be happy in your relationships. Have a win-win mentality. At the end of the day, the people in our lives are the most important people. Relationships are the key to success. Always remember that the people in your life influence your behavior. Generally, if the people around you are positive and successful, you will become more positive and successful. If people around you complain all the time and think that the world owes them everything, you will become that way also. If people around you are intelligent, you will become more intelligent too. You become like the people who surround you.

Exercise – Take Control of Your Relationships

It takes some work to find the right people and build quality relationships, but if you keep your goal in mind, it will be easier because you will not compromise. Every experience, good or bad, is a lesson so do not take stumbles personally but stay focused on your path to meeting the right people who will help you become successful.

Who is your role model? Who has achieved what you are trying to do? Once you find these people, you should read their work, biographies, and learn how they think and work. Find out what challenges they had to overcome and how they did it. Then model their behavior and be aware of your own changes while you are going through this exercise. I am convinced that you will be impressed with your progress. That's what you need to move on with your own goals and come up with successful strategies to achieve them. ACTION is the key word here because without it nothing ever happens. However, first, you need to be aware of the people who already exist in your life and find out what purpose they serve.

In your journal, answer these questions:

1   Who are the people I spend the most time with? How do I feel when I am around these people? Optimistic, inspired, motivated, etc.

2   Do these people complain about their life or they are responsible and accountable for what happens to them?

3   Do these people have a growth mindset – always learning and improving themselves or do they have a fixed mindset – thinking they cannot improve, that talent is enough to achieve success or that their problems make it impossible for them to succeed?.

4   Do these people enjoy their work? Do they have a passion for it?

What answers did you get? Now you know what to do to change every negative into a positive? If you want a positive environment, then you need to have positive people around, and only you can make that happen.

Coaching Moment

We cannot achieve anything on our own. Associating with the right people can help advance your career, improve your quality of life and make you a better person. It's a great feeling. I shared my story with you about finding my first mentors, Dimitri and Sharon and later, Joan. I wanted to surround myself with amazing people – smart, educated, positive, determined, caring and loving. However, to attract high-quality people I needed to become one myself. And I did. You can do the same. You need to show your mentors why they should invest time in you, for them to see the value in you.

Who Am I?

"Knowing yourself is the beginning of all wisdom"

—ARISTOTLE

We all want success, love, health, and happiness; it is just human nature. Before you can have those things for yourself, however, you need to know who you really are. The Scottish philosopher David Hume said that each of us is born with no thoughts or ideas, a term he calls *tabula rasa* or blank slate. Therefore, every person's mind is the sum of everything she or he learned from birth onward. Who you are is the result of your experiences, from your earliest life until today. In the next section, we will discuss the importance of *self-concept*, the degree to which how you see yourself determines how you feel and what you do. It is then imperative that you take a moment to apply the following self-analysis and learn more about who you think you are. Are you ready?

In your journal, write down ten words or sentences that describe who you are as a person. For instance, you may describe your social roles such as a student, spouse, son, friend, brother, daughter or physical features such as beautiful, skinny, short, tall. You could even describe character traits such as smart, stupid, curious or optimistic, pessimistic, critical, confident, energetic, or shy. Alternatively, you may want to describe yourself regarding belief systems such as Christian, vegetarian, atheist, and so on. Be brutally honest with yourself. This exercise is for your eyes only and you can only affect change if you are willing to be honest.

Trait Type	Examples	Your Traits
Social Roles	Student	
	Spouse	
	Son	
	Friend	
	Brother	
	Daughter	
Physical Traits	Beautiful	
	Unattractive	
	Skinny	
	Short	
	Tall	
	Overweight	
Character Traits	Smart	
	Curious	
	Optimistic	
	Pessimistic	
	Critical	
	Confident	
	Energetic	
	Shy	

Trait Type	Examples	Your Traits
Belief Traits	Religious	
	Vegan	
	Feminist	
	Atheist	
	Republican	
	Democrat	

Now that you have ten words or sentences that describe you, go ahead and rank them in order of importance, assigning a number to each one from one as the most important to ten as the least important. Then create "I am" statements that describe who you are, listing several of the traits in order of their importance to you. Here are two examples;

I am a feminist, healthy, confident, beautiful and smart

I am religious, overweight, pessimistic, and unattractive

Who Am I?
1
2
3
4
5
6
7
8
9
10

When you look at the words and phrases that you wrote down, do you see two or more that have something in common? Carefully examine your choices and think about how they apply to the following:

Self-Concept

The exercise you just completed gives insight about your ***self-concept***[7]**, which is the way we see or define ourselves.** For some people, beauty and physical appearance are the most important. For others, higher education and achievements are important. It is imperative to know how and why you perceive yourself the way you do because it affects who you become as an adult and how you will live your life today as well as in the future. You will also be able to make changes once you understand that your happiness is related to how you see and feel about yourself. Remember that we are born without a self-concept. It is wholly constructed from our experiences.

Self-Esteem

Self-esteem plays an important role in how we value ourselves. Simply, **self-esteem**[8] **is how worthwhile you think you are.** This then determines the intensity level with which you live your life. The higher your self-esteem, the more motivated and inspired you are to do your best at everything you attempt to accomplish. Therefore, it is imperative that you understand it and evaluate it. *Self-esteem is a learned behavior*. Poor self-esteem can be unlearned if you chose to do so. I am not saying that it is easy. However, it is possible to face your fears, learn from your experiences and continue to observe and adjust your behavior to achieve desired results.

We are not born with self-esteem. It develops because of social interaction and perceived social comparisons. For instance, think about someone who helped improve your self-esteem by making you feel accepted, loved and appreciated. Now, think about someone who diminished your self-esteem – maybe someone in your family who criticized you all the time or a teacher who did not support your efforts.

Reflecting on what we have covered so far, you can probably identify those who made a positive influence in your early life and those who did not. If you were supported and loved, then you developed a high sense of self-worth. If you were often criticized and judged, then you may feel less valuable, less capable, and less worthy of love. Usually, people with low self-esteem react in self-defense or a self-destructive manner. They get upset easily, take things personally and often they lose their sense of self. These behaviors are learned from negative childhood experiences. *The good news is that you have the power within you to change who you are and who you want to become.* There are many tools available to help you improve your self-esteem including, books, workshops, and perhaps even counseling or coaching. The importance of self-esteem cannot be overstated. It is one of the most important keys to your self-development so it is worth taking the necessary time and effort to assure that you have high self-esteem. It is the foundation upon which your successes will be built.

Self-Efficacy

Self-efficacy[9] refers to a person's belief about his or her ability to achieve a goal. If you really want to and believe you can achieve a particular task, you will work harder, be less distracted and less likely to give up. If you are not confident in your abilities, then you will find excuses as to why you failed. Your efforts and hard work completing a task are directly related to your belief that you can do it. Always think "Yes **I CAN**" and then figure it out how to get it done.

When I started college, I was anxious and afraid, but I believed I could do it. Even though my English was not perfect, I didn't have family support, and wasn't familiar with the education system of my new country, I believed I could do it. This belief allowed me to schedule my work, cope with unexpected challenges, ask for help when I needed it, and learn from mistakes. Having self-confidence and believing I could do it allowed me to face challenges head on. I learned to think of skills and strategies to work smarter and not harder.

As with me, with every new accomplishment, you will become more confident. You will become more aware of your feelings, body, mind, and soul. You will no longer rely on other people's approval to do the things you need and love to do. At last, you will be able to trust yourself to voice your true opinions and feelings and make your needs known. You will become responsible and accountable for your own successes and failures. When things are not going well it's okay to feel sorry for yourself for a little while, that's fine. Then get up and keep going because that is the only way to a better life and greater happiness.

Life Values

What are your most important values?

To know how you want to live your life requires that you truly understand your values. Knowing your most important values will give you clarity and awareness to focus on what matters most to you.

Every life value is significant, but it's helpful to prioritize them from the most important to the least important. Prioritizing values allows you to *design your life* around them and to spend your time and energy accordingly. You do not want to waste your time on things that do not give you the results you want. It is important that we not get distracted and drift away from our course of action. Values act as a compass to redirect us and keep us on track.

First step – Find Your Values

First, try to relax and make sure you are in a quiet place without distractions. Use the table below to identify which values are the most important to you. Evaluate which words hold the most meaning to you, and which are unimportant. Then, 'rate' each word as most important, somewhat important, or not important with an *X* in the appropriate box. If you don't see a specific value/ principle here, go ahead and add your own. Do not worry about the order of importance at this point; we will do that next. For now, just focus on finding the values that are the most important to you:

Categories	Value	Most Important	Somewhat Important	Not Important
Personal	Self-empowerment			
	Security			
	Intelligence			
	Self-discipline			
	Independence			
	Knowledge			
	Lifelong Learning			
	Open-mindedness			
	Fairness			
	Freedom			
	Thoughtfulness			
	Responsibility			
	Punctuation			
	Determination			
	Persistence			
	Health			
	Other			
	Other			
Character	Confidence			
	Happiness			
	Love			
	Peace of Mind			
	Simplicity			
	Being True to Yourself			
	Fulfilment			
	Spirituality			
	Other			
	Other			

Categories	Value	Most Important	Somewhat Important	Not Important
Social	Fun			
	Adventure			
	Making a difference			
	Helping Others			
	Spreading Good Karma			
	Connection with Others			
	Couple-relationship			
	Other			
Career	Communication			
	Success			
	Professionalism			
	Wealth			
	Other			
	Other			

Now, you should have a clear idea of the things that you value the most. If you have too many values in the 'most important category, reevaluate them until only ten are left. Once you have that, you're ready to move on to the next part of this exercise.

Next step – Prioritize Your Values

Now, look at all of the values that fall under the most important category and begin to prioritize them in order of importance from 1 to 10, using the space below. You may ask yourself these questions: *What motivates me? What do I want to change? What do I want more of in my life?* You need to answer these questions as you work out your list of most important values. There are no right or wrong values you live by as long as you are happy and those values give you what you need. For example, if health is the most important value to you, then it becomes your number one value. Likewise, if money is the most important value to you then it becomes your first priority. Repeat the process and go down the list until you have your values in order of importance. If you came up with your own values that weren't included in the list above, feel free to use them as well.

As you will find, this is not an easy process. However, by prioritizing your values consciously, you'll be able to make informed decisions that will give you the best results. Feel free to reassess and reexamine your list of values and do not be afraid to change them or reorder them as you move on in life. Again, there are no right or wrong answers as you are defining the answer that is right for you. You may want to use a verb with each most important value so you can see how you will use it in an actionable step.

My Most Important Values
1
2
3
4
5
6
7
8
9
10

Now that you have prioritized your values, you should have a clear idea of which category your strongest values fall under. Using the chart below, tally up the values you have under each category. This exercise will allow you to understand which area of your life is your primary focus and what areas are less important.

Personal	Character	Social	Career

Now, look at the chart below and place a dot on it to indicate how each category scored. Depending on your answers, your graph may come out balanced, or heavily centered around a particular category. Either way is perfectly fine. The point here is to gain a better understanding of what matters to you the most. That way, you can start planning your future around the things that are important to you. You will finally begin to live an authentic life by living your life by your own rules. Living your life by design NOT by chance.

As they say, where the time goes, the energy flows. That is why it is imperative that you spend time on things that align with your values in order to create the life you want. The key here is balance. Try to spread out your energy evenly over your most important values to get the most out of your time.

Keep in mind that time is a finite resource. If we spend our time today on things that don't make us happy or improve our lives, then we have wasted our time. That is time that we cannot get it back. It is important that we spend our time on what we value.

Let's go over some examples to illustrate. Then we can use the chart to make inferences about possible goals or life changes.

For instance, you might have come up with this list:

1 Self-Empowerment (Personal)

2 Success (Career)

3 Happiness (Character)

4 Health (Personal)

5 Adventure (Social)

6 Wealth (Career)

7 Professionalism (Career)

8 Helping others (Social)

9 Love (Character)

10 Communication (Career)

What can we infer from these results? Knowing what a person values tell us a great deal about that person's behavior and how they live their life. The list on the left shows us what particular trait you value the most, while the graph on the right tells us in what area of your life you spend the most energy. Using both list and graph gives us the ability to see your motivations as a whole. We will go over each individually, and then look at what they mean together. Let us get started.

First, we will examine the top value on the list, *self-empowerment*, which is the purpose of this book. Answering this means you likely hold independence and self-reliance above other traits and wish to keep full control of your life.

Traits that someone who highly values self-empowerment may possess:

- ✓ They make choices according to their values

- ✓ They live by their own rather than someone else's expectations and belief systems

- ✓ They're always pushing for more and competing with themselves

- ✓ They define their own "success" and never blame anyone else for success or failures

- ✓ They are open-minded and aware of reality

- ✓ They feel free to change their thinking to fit new values as situations change

Now, what information can you gain by looking at the chart on the right? As you can see, this list is fairly balanced, with career aspirations taking the lead. Given these results, we can ascertain that you highly value your career, whatever that might be, but also want balance in other aspects of your life. If you want to be successful in your top category, you will plan your goals with concrete action steps geared toward advancing your career. If you place career above the other categories, you should ask yourself the following questions when setting goals. *Am I happy in my career? What area of my career could be better? Am I paid what I am worth?* When you have your answers, you will know where to start and you are on your way to figuring out what to do.

Yes, it is vital that you understand what your results mean separately, but it is just as important to know how your values can work in harmony.

In this example, you value self-empowerment but also aspire to succeed in your career. You will feel the most satisfaction by aligning your core values towards a cohesive goal. To feel both empowered and successful in your career, you will have to work towards being independent in your field. This could mean starting your own business, or even 'climbing the ladder,' so to speak, of a reputable establishment.

Now let us look at someone with a different set of values and see what happens:

1 Wealth

2 Connection with Others

3 Making a Difference

4 Lifelong Learning

5 Helping Others

6 Fulfilment

7 Peace of Mind

8 Freedom

9 Fun

10 Spreading Good Karma

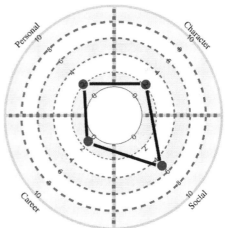

What can we now say about someone's lifestyle and behaviors knowing that their top value is wealth? Apparently, this person prefers wealth to things like lifelong learning and helping others. It is fine for someone to want wealth. However, how it is acquired makes the difference between focusing the time and energy creating wealth at the expense of sacrificing the other values such as love, having free time, relationships and so on. Likewise, you may wonder – *what is wealth and how much of it do I need to be happy. Why do I need this much? What sacrifices am I making and is it worth it?* These questions need answers as you work out your list of most important values. There is not a right or a wrong way of determining which value you live by as long as you are happy and those values give you what you need in life.

Now let's examine the chart above on the right. Go back and look at it again. As you can see, this chart is more unbalanced than the first one. Having an unbalanced chart is not a bad thing. It only means that certain values are more important over others. This person enjoys helping others and giving back to their community, as well as having a little fun.

What inferences can we make when we take into account this person's value for wealth and their social aspirations? Well, this person would benefit greatly from finding something that fits into the social category, while also adding to their financial wealth. This might mean getting into for-profit charities. It may be necessary to switch companies to one that gives back to the community or even starting your own business helping others. The possibilities are endless, but the point here is for you use these examples and figure your own path based on what you value the most in order to live a happy life. After all, even if a career is very important to you, what is the point of working long hours and not having any free time to enjoy with family and friends?

Informed Decisions

Now that you know and understand your values, it will be easier to make informed decisions that will allow you to achieve what you want out of life. Whether it is moving away for a job, pursuing a relationship, getting a higher education degree, getting married, losing weight, or traveling the world, the answers to these questions will allow you to make decisions that are in harmony with your values. For all of us, the ultimate goal is to be happy. It is therefore necessary that you live your life in alignment with your values and goals. If, by default, you live your life in misalignment, you will lose your sense of integrity and respect for yourself. You will not be happy. You do not want that. You are powerful enough to make choices for yourself that will empower you to live a fulfilled, value-driven, happy life. You don't want to feel the regrets that some people have at the end of life. They wish they had pursued their passions, spent more time with family and lived their life doing what they wanted and not what society expected of them.

Indeed, it is all about choices. What are you going to choose today that will make your tomorrow better? In the following chapters, we will discuss the POWER of choices and how they create long lasting success or failure. When we understand ourselves, we understand the connection between the choices we make and the life we have. We will seek out information to expand our knowledge and apply it consciously to improve our lives.

Exercise – The Road to a Happy Life

You have explored the values that make you happy and give you purpose in life. Now answer these questions in your journal:

1   What is most important in your life?

2   Why are those things important to you?

3   What does it mean to have a good life?

4   What makes you happy?

5   What does it mean to be a good person?

6   Imagine that you are writing your own obituary, how would you like to be remembered?

Coaching Moment

You have ONE life and deserve to enjoy it and be happy. We all want happiness, and in order to find yours, you need to understand your values and who you are as a person. To become successful, you need to love what you do. If you work ten hours a day doing something you do not enjoy you will never be happy. It is time to take some risks and pursue your values and passions. Find your passion and then figure out a way to market yourself and get paid for it. Currently, the possibilities are endless, so there is no reason why you should spend your career doing something you do not enjoy. You can do better and you deserve better.

> *"Choose a job you love and you will never have to work a day in your life."*
>
> —Confucius

Not *All* Knowledge Is Power

"You can lose everything you own but your educated mind no one can take it from you. With it you can start your life over."

—Dad

Now that you have examined your values and have a better understanding of who you are and what makes you happy, we will discuss the type of knowledge you need to improve your life. Luckily, we live in extraordinary times. Never before have we been able to turn on the computer and access ANY information we want. It's easy to find the information you seek in today's world, but putting that information to use is up to you.

If there is a particular skill, you need to work on, take the time to find some classes you can take. You would be surprised to find that there are tons of websites offering free and affordable priced courses. Whatever your ambitions, whatever skills you need to learn, most likely there is a course for it. All you need is ACTION.

To become empowered, you need to become a lifelong learner. Yes, you CAN. First, you need to BELIEVE that the difference between you and other people who may be ahead of you financially, spiritually, professionally or otherwise, is that they know and do the things that you do not yet know and do. They are accountable and responsible for their lives. You too can LEARN what you need in order to change your life for the better, just as they did, and just as I did. The question is, are you READY to change your life?

First, reassess where you are. You need to be honest with yourself in order to create the life you deserve to have. After all, you only have this one life so why not do the best you can to enjoy it? To get started, you need to become reflective. You need to be consciously aware of your life as it is NOW. You need to be in touch with your feelings, needs and wants and acknowledge why you feel the way you do. Then you will be able to make informed decisions about what you should do next. This chapter will help you begin your lifelong journey to self-empowerment.

Let me repeat: you need to be honest with yourself if you are serious about changing your life. No one will do it for you. You have the power within you to create the life you know you want. Do not wait any longer. You do not have time to wait.

In fact, it's a bit late. Begin your journey to empowerment today.

I am here to support you so start your journey to empowering yourself TODAY!

The Importance of Education

*"Education is transformational. It changes
lives. That is why people work so hard to
become educated and why education has always
been the key to the American Dream."*

—Condoleezza Rice

*"I believe that the rights of women and girls
is the unfinished business of the 21st century."*

—Hillary Clinton

Pursuing a college education has been my goal as long as I can remember: it was my gateway to freedom. When you grow up as I did, the urgency to educate yourself becomes paramount.

Returning to my life-story, it had now been three years since I arrived in the United States. Since I had been here, I changed jobs several times and met extraordinary people along the way. My command of the English language had improved enough to begin college. I did not have time to wait.

My expectation was that college life was supposed to be exciting and challenging at the same time. However, I found myself overwhelmed, questioning whether pursuing college was the right decision. In fact, I thought all college instructors were supposed to be supportive and inspiring, motivating their students to push themselves and to believe in their own abilities. While many of them were supportive and inspirational, like Dr. Black and

Dr. Morris, there was one instructor, let's call him Mr. Negative, who, after grading my first assignment in his class, told me I should rethink my decision to pursue a college education. I did not expect that everyone would support my academic goals, but this was my teacher whose job was to inspire and motivate me to work even harder and never give up on my dream. As you can imagine, I was flabbergasted. *I quickly was reminded that when life gives you lemons, make lemonade.* I saw that I needed to become mentally and emotionally strong if I was to face such setbacks and not let them deter me from my goals. Something extraordinary happened as a result: I knew I wanted to become a teacher and that when I became a teacher, it would be my goal to inspire and motivate students to achieve what they did not think possible. I vowed never to treat a student the way Mr. Negative had treated me. I used his insensitivity to reinforce my armor against those who might doubt me and made a promise to myself to encourage rather than discourage others.

Nothing deterred me from following my dream to pursue a college education. I had to work during the day to make a living, so I signed up for night courses instead; just as I had done to finish high school in Romania. Luckily, my mentors were supportive during this time and helped me with scheduling work around my classes. Nonetheless, working full-time during the day and going to college full-time at night was challenging, complicated, and overwhelming.

As time went by, I started to achieve success in my classes and became a little more assured of my ability to excel. As my confidence level increased, I continued to work even harder. Even though I was not afraid of hard work, I did not want to spend all my time studying, pulling all-nighters and stressing myself out, which is what I did at first. Despite my satisfactory progress, I was not happy with my personal life. I did not have time for myself just to enjoy and have fun. I had no life outside of work and school. I was working harder than ever, but I began to feel that I was not being fully effective. That is why I decided to invest time reading and watching videos about people who had to overcome similar challenges. I knew there had to be a better way to get things done and live my life.

I decided that spending endless hours studying and writing papers, stressing out and getting annoyed, all the while working full time was making me unhappy. I am an optimistic person by nature, so giving up had never been an option, but I was miserable with the way things were. Thus, I started seriously looking for a better way. I read countless books on a wide range of topics, from time management, productivity, self-development, and study skills, to psychology and sociology, with many other genres in between. I began researching and reading about successful people and their success strategies. I learned how to use S.M.A.R.T[10]. goals, which we will discuss in a later chapter.

First of all, I had to accept that to change my life, I had to change my thinking once again. I decided to design a success plan and implement the new skills and strategies that I had learned. I had to work both smarter and harder. Once I settled on a set of strategies, nothing stopped me from sailing thru my classes to complete my associate degree in two years with a 3.1 GPA. Not too bad for someone still learning English.

Did you know that only 5% of full-time students graduate in two years with an associate degree?

47

I am proud to belong to this group, and it is a lesson and a reminder to anyone out there that may question their ability to achieve a college degree, or any goal they set for themselves.

Alternatively, if someone tells you to change your plans because they think you do not have the ability to do it (as Mr. Negative told me), don't listen, and just keep on going. It's better to try and fail and learn from it than not try and have regrets. If I could do it, anyone can! Do not worry if you are afraid. I understand. I have been there and have overcome that fear, and I will show you how you too can overcome your fears. Keep in mind that fear is just in our heads. Brush it aside and replace it with determination.

I was not about to stop my education after my associate degree. I had worked hard to develop my strategies for success and felt like I was on my way. Without taking a break, I immediately transferred to the University of Central Florida in Orlando. There I completed my Bachelor's and Master's Degrees in sociology with a minor in political science in 3.7 years.

Did you know that only about 36% of full-time college students graduate on time[11]?

In the summer of 2005, immediately after my graduation, I decided to move on to yet another challenge. I donated everything I had and traveled from Orlando to New York. I asked a friend to hold onto what was left of my belongings and purchased a one-way ticket to London, UK. I spent the next three months traveling the world.

I came back a new person with new perspectives, ideas, and purpose in life. I had decided to go back to school, pursue a doctor of education degree, and dedicate my life to service and empowering women and girls everywhere. This time I was more confident than ever that I could do it. After all, I already had a master's degree, so I knew it was possible, but now I had to ask myself whether I still had the determination and resilience to do it. The answer was a decisive YES.

As you recall, my parents didn't have the opportunity to pursue an education. Therefore, I wanted to break all barriers, not only for my family and myself but also for others who were in the same situation and did not believe they could achieve their dreams. I wanted to be their spokesperson, inspiration, and role model to show them how to get it done. We need to empower ourselves to reach our full potential and live a purposeful, value–driven, happy life. I know that college is not for everyone; however, every person needs some education, whether it is formal or informal, to remain relevant in their field and to pursue opportunities that make them happy.

*"Women and girls should determine their own future,
no matter where they're born."*

—Melinda Gates

Four years later, I graduated with an education specialist degree, and a doctor of education leadership degree; it was one of the best moments of my life! I dedicated my achievement to my mom and all the women around the world who did not have an education – this is for you! I knew I made Mom and Dad proud and changed our family legacy. Now I wanted to teach and make a difference in others' lives. I wanted to inspire and motivate people of all ages, especially women, to inspire them to believe that anything is possible with a vision, passion, courage, a plan, hard work, perseverance, and self-belief.

While it is important to remember where we come from and that we cannot change our past, it is our responsibility to change the present for a better future. We deserve to be happy.

Become a Lifelong Learner

> *"Let us pick our books and pencils.*
> *They are our most powerful weapon."*
>
> —Malala Yousafzai

Lifelong learning is no longer a choice for women like you and me. You and I need to understand that life is moving and changing quickly, and a commitment to keep up our skills and improve our knowledge-set is paramount.

We all want to be successful, financially independent, healthy and happy. The reality is that it CAN be done; it is possible now more than ever before. Some people seem to hope for the best and just wait for change to happen by the process of osmosis. The truth is that is not how success works. Hope, while necessary, does not get us there. If we want a better life, then we need to make up our mind and make it happen. Our thoughts and choices determine our happiness.

Be honest with yourself right now. You are where you are today because of the choices you have made, either consciously or unconsciously. If you are not happy in any area of your life, then you need to have an honest discussion with yourself and decide finally that today it is the time to change the way things are in your life.

The work you do today is a consequence of your choices, which reflect your qualifications and skills. Increasing your knowledge allows you to make informed decisions and be more in control of your life.

Exercise – Empower Your Mind

Take a moment to write in your journal what you need to learn and study to improve your skill set and become more competitive in the global economy. For instance, you could write:

I will enroll in a communication or public speaking course because I want to become a more effective speaker.

I will enroll in a negotiation course to learn how to negotiate successfully.

I will enroll in a defense class because I want to learn to defend myself.

I will learn a second language in order to advance my career opportunities.

I will enroll in a finance course to learn how to manage my finances.

I will enroll in a self-confidence course.

Armed with your questions, move on to research. Open your laptop and fire up that search engine or go to the library or bookstore. You can easily find local instructors in a wide range of fields if you only look. Make sure that you find the right one, however. Be sure to check credentials and authenticity before dedicating your valuable time by signing up for any courses. Again, there are many free lessons that you can access online. YouTube is a great place to start.

> *"The quality of a person's life will be determined*
> *by the depth of their commitment to excellence,*
> *no matter what their chosen field."*
>
> —Vince Lombardi

Commitment is critical to your success and signing up for a course requires that you dedicate time and energy. I often tell my students to question their motives for taking a particular college class that requires them to sit in for three hours at the time. A learning environment is a place where students have the freedom to find out who they are, what they want to study and how to make the best out of the time and money they spend on their education. At the end of class, I ask them to write in their journal what they learned and how they can use that information in the real world. If it is not applicable to the real world, then we have wasted our time, and we need to revisit our objectives.

Likewise, I emphasize that being a student is about learning and growing as a person and contributing to the community and the world. They should not be concerned with what their peers think of them, especially when they stumble or get a lower grade.

Instead, they should work harder and improve their skills and abilities to successfully compete and integrate into the global economy while being able to live a decent, meaningful life.

You too should ask yourself at the end of the day – *did I achieve my goals today? What have I learned? What can I do differently to ensure a better tomorrow?* It is important to live with intention and purpose each day if you want to achieve your goals and make your life count. Taking action is the key word here for without it nothing ever happens.

Coaching Moment

I use an MIT (most important things) – ROT (return on time) system to make sure I complete the most important things or goals and the time I spent working on them was well worth it. At the end of the day, just as I ask you and my students I too reflect and write down how my day went and what I need to do to ensure a more productive tomorrow.

How to Become a Lifelong Learner

1 Read every day

> *"Read 500 pages every day. That's how knowledge works.*
> *It builds up like compound interest."*

—WARREN BUFFETT

Warren Buffet, Bill Gates, Oprah Winfrey, Mark Cuban, Madeleine Albright, and many others make reading a major part

53

of their daily lifestyle. Yes, they read a lot. Every Day. Successful people read every day and are very selective about what they read. They read to become educated, not entertained. For example, the author of *Rich Habits: The Daily Success Habits of Wealthy Individuals, (Corley, 2005)*[12] found that people with an annual income over $160,000 read educational books, self-improvement, biographies, business strategies, leadership and empowerment books. People who make $40,000 or less read very little and when they do, they read tabloids and magazines.

You need to adopt the reading habit if you have not already. You cannot afford to spend your time reading tabloids and watching reality television shows, both of which waste your time. You need to read self-improvement books and specialized knowledge books. Again, go to your local bookstore, get a cup of coffee, grab a few specialized knowledge books and let yourself become immersed in this newfound knowledge. You will be amazed at the transformation.

2 Go to School – it is always open

Successful people never stop learning. They continuously look for opportunities to increase their value in the market place. Unfortunately, the education system is not always teaching you how to live your life according to your values and how to pursue your passions and happiness. Therefore, once again you need to take action and find out the skills, mindsets, and environment you need to create a life that you will enjoy living.

What skills do you need to advance your career or to open your own business?

Go ahead and enroll in a class today that offers the skills you need. Yes, you deserve to invest in yourself, and there is no price tag for that. One thing I learned early on was that there is no price too high when it comes to investing in myself. You should do the same. Identify your career goal, the skills you need to get there, and then sign up for the course that offers those skills, webinars or meetings where you might find someone to inspire and motivate you. You should be spending every minute of your day intentionally. Ask yourself this question – what is the value of how I am spending my time at this moment? If there is no value, then you need to be doing something else that has value.

Earlier I introduced my simple formula for making sure I spend my time wisely – MIT = ROT – Most Important Things = Return On my Time. I make sure each day I am working on "the most important things," and at the end of the day, I analyze the results or value I get based on the time I spent. Was it worth it? Do I need to adjust anything? How can I get the most value and spend as little time as possible? To be highly effective in life, it is important for you to put the right effort on the right things.

3   Surround Yourself with Great People

> *"Great minds discuss ideas. Average minds discuss events. Small minds discuss people."*
>
> —ELEANOR ROOSEVELT

There are people who inspire you to become a better person and empower you to make the changes you need to be more productive. To attract good quality people you need to have a positive energy and self-confidence. You have to be honest. Be real. It is the only way you will live an authentic life that you'll be proud off. Surround yourself with optimistic, driven, and confident people and you will be happier, less stressed, inspired and energized. Wouldn't you agree that there is enough phoniness in the world and to have real people around you is priceless? Strive to be "real," and you will attract honest people to you.

What Is Knowledge

> *"Believe nothing, no matter where you read it,*
> *or who said it, no matter if I said it…*
> *Unless it agrees with your own reason*
> *and your own common sense."*

—BUDDHA

Knowledge is power, as the saying goes. I used to say it all the time until I realized that knowledge on its own has NO value. It is about HOW we interpret and use the knowledge that makes it powerful and useful. Think about it, if you read about how to manage your time effectively without practicing and benefiting from it then just reading the article would not solve your time management problem. Therefore, knowledge is information acquired by experience, reading, experimentation and thought processes such as visualization and critical thinking. Once you are aware of the knowledge you possess and know HOW to use it effectively to better your life then yes, knowledge is powerful because your critical thinking ability and application gives it its power. It is your critical thinking ability, planning, organizing and applying the knowledge to solve a problem that makes it compelling.

These days it is easier than ever to acquire knowledge about any subject of interest. All you need to do is locate the information you need, study it and then apply it. For instance, if you need to learn how to communicate effectively or learn how to invest in mutual funds, you can go online and sign up for free or small fee online courses from prestigious universities such as MIT[13] or Columbia university[14]. Likewise, you can enroll in a paid course, which will count towards credit or a degree you may want to pursue. Of course, this requires effort, planning, dedication, and persistence. There is no success without hard work. However, if you want it badly enough, you have the ability to achieve anything.

Accomplished women are lifelong learners, always seeking out new information, skills, and systems to learn and apply knowledge. They embrace technology, whether they like it or not. They find mentors and role models, and they surround themselves with people who will support their goals. These women are passionate about their work because they love what they do. They are intentional about how they spend their time and are effective in managing their multiple roles. They are EMPOWERED. They know what they want, and they go after it. No one will stop them or change their minds. WHY NOT YOU? You deserve to be EMPOWERED.

"To be yourself in a world that is constantly trying to make you something else is the greatest accomplishment."

—RALPH WALDO EMERSON

Exercise – Accept Praise and Sharpen Your skills

Many women do not feel comfortable talking about their accomplishments and expertise and do not give themselves the credit they deserve. You need to become your biggest cheerleader because no one else will do it for you. The more skills and knowledge you have, the more you have to offer in any given situation. Think about it, you see someone at a meeting or in a store and engage in small talk – what are you going to say? When you have knowledge on various topics, it is easier and more fun to talk with other people and network. You never know who you will meet – it could be your next client, friend, employer or mentor. It is crucial that you make sure people perceive you as an empowered woman – educated, worldly confident, and ready to serve and make a difference.

In your journal, write a list of ten skills you want to learn over the next six months. Think about skills that would help with your life values – health, wealth, spirituality, finance, relationships, and love. Start with one skill at the time. Use the S.M.A.R.T. goal setting formula and the MIT-ROT formula, and you will be in control of your time and of your life.

I am always learning something new – I always challenge my mind, my body and my soul. For example, these are some of things I pursued or currently doing:

- ✓ Joined Toastmaster to improve my public speaking skills – I even won "the best speech award"

- ✓ Meditation and yoga

- ✓ Learned money management

✓ Learned to build a website

✓ Learned to podcast

✓ Learned another language

✓ Trained and ran a marathon (26.2 miles)

✓ Learned to coach and empower people

✓ Learned to manage my emotions and not be reactive

✓ Learned to manage and use time and energy according to my plans

✓ Developed and designed online courses

✓ Learned to take time out to relax without feeling guilty

✓ Learned to say NO to people who didn't add value to my life

✓ Learned to let go of perfection

✓ Learned to be happy

✓ Learning to swim

✓ Learning to play guitar

✓ The list continues….

Coaching Moment

We have this one amazing life to do great things and make a difference. The truth is that you have within you everything you need to change and design the life you want for yourself. The Law of Substitution says, "*Your mind can hold only one thought at the time, positive or negative. You can substitute a positive thought for a negative thought whenever you choose.*" Fear is in our minds but seems very real. I know because I have overcome many fears in my life and right now, I am working on learning to swim. Getting over my fear of deep water was a great accomplishment. Now I am taking swimming classes and cannot believe I did not do it sooner. We create fear but as soon as we move towards it and overcome it by becoming confident, we realize how much stronger we really are. Do not let fear tell you what you can and cannot do. Acquire the skills you need to become empowered and do not worry about what others think or say. Give yourself permission to change and create the life you want according to your values and passion. Do not waste one more day or minute being a victim or feeling sorry for yourself. You are better than that and you know it.

What It Means To Be Empowered

*"When you know yourself, you are empowered.
Only then you are in control of your life."*

I am not afraid. I was born to do this."

—Joan Of Arc

To be empowered means to be in control of your life. YOU have the ability to live the life of your dreams and whether this happens or not begins with your thoughts and beliefs. Your mind is your best asset to achieve what you want in life. Empowered women think differently – they have a mindset that helps them stay motivated to reach for goals that others may find difficult to achieve. What do people like Oprah Winfrey, Melinda Gates, Madeline Albright, Malala Yousafzai, Sheryl Sandberg, Laura Dekker, Ellen DeGeneres, Michelle Obama, Nadia Comaneci, Angela Merkel and so many other extraordinary women have in common? Simply put, they developed a mindset for success. They are empowered. They are in control. They do not take NO for an answer. They believe in their abilities and are determined to do whatever it takes to achieve their goals. WHY NOT YOU? You too deserve to become empowered.

Today's world moves at a fast pace, and the many commitments we make and responsibilities we have can easily distract us from who we are as people. That and the fact that many women self-lessly put the needs of others ahead of their own can make us feel lost and purposeless. The decision to put yourself first and strive for your achievements is entirely up to you. There is no point in reaching the phase where you regret your life choices. Instead, choose self-empowerment. After all, when you are happy, every-one around you is happy.

What is self-empowerment, you ask? As stated briefly in the introduction, self-empowerment means you are in control of your life. It means awareness of your beliefs, behaviors, attitudes, and expectations. It is about self-control and self-discipline. It means setting goals and making the necessary changes to optimize the results. It means being confident and having the courage to make mistakes and to learn from them.

Are you ready to take the first step towards self-empowerment, which is taking care of yourself, your needs and your priorities? If you're reading this book and made it this far then the answer is likely 'yes.' You know that you deserve to live a better life. You also know that the ability to achieve anything you ever wanted resides within you. It is important that you stop waiting around for things to change or for someone else to change things for you. You are the designer of all the successes, or failures, in your life. Your actions define you and the choices you make every day are reflected in your life.

"If you paint in your mind a picture of
bright and happy expectations, you put yourself
into a condition conducive to your goals."

—NORMAN VINCENT PEALE

If you are just starting out on the path to empowerment, you may want to start working on your life one goal at a time. You may seek financial independence, to become a better time manager, to achieve educational success, to travel, or maybe to lose weight and get into better physical shape. Be aware that about 20% of us will ever do anything about our goals and passions; even less than 20% will ever achieve them, in fact, only about 8% of people achieve their goals[15]. Indeed, it is not easy or simple, but we know one thing; it is possible. It does not help to just talk about it. You have to do it. That said why is it so difficult to achieve success and be happy. Why only about 8% of people achieve their goals?

If we are honest, it seems that many people would rather be entertained than empowered. They feel stuck in a cycle of work just to pay the bills, and when they get home from a long day, they would rather watch television than do something productive. Nevertheless, that's where you can be different. Being successful can become more important to you than being entertained.

I will show you that it is possible to become empowered and live a good life. I have described the obstacles I encountered and overcame. You will have obstacles too. But if I could do it, so can you. You deserve to be the best that you can be and who better to teach you how to become empowered than someone who has already done it?

Free yourself from anything that holds you back

Declare yourself empowered in every area of your life

You are never a victim. Kill the old self. Reinvent the new self

You are a winner

You are the creator of your success

Empowered Mindset

> *"Nothing is either good or bad,*
> *but thinking makes it so."*

—SHAKESPEARE

Your mindset includes the beliefs, values, fears, abilities, talents, successes, and failures, which affect your decisions and experiences you have.

For instance, have you wondered why some people are more successful in their careers and their personal lives than others are? Do you think it is because they are smarter than you or me? No. Intelligence definitely contributes to success, but it is their mindset and habits that ultimately allow someone to achieve results. For instance, personal characteristics such as hard work, time and energy management, support, determination, persistence, goal planning, and continuous learning, are more important than intelligence and talent alone. People with an empowered mindset never stop sharpening their skills and learning new ones.

Whether it is school, life or career, successful people think differently – they have a growth mindset, or as I call it, an "I CAN DO IT" mindset. A fixed mindset, on the other hand, prevents people from taking chances and from believing that their hard work and persistence will determine their level of success. People with a fixed mindset believe that successful people have "innate abilities," "success genes," or have gotten all the breaks. This could not be further from the truth. Achieving success requires each one of us to be willing to change our circumstances if we are not happy or satisfied. We cannot expect extraordinary things to happen without change.

The first thing you need to do is to raise your expectations and awareness. Don't be satisfied with being average. The world is full of mediocre and average people who are more likely to complain about their circumstances than try to change them.

If you want to be above average, to be amazing, you cannot do ordinary work. Create opportunities for yourself to have a great life. Challenge yourself and raise your expectations. You have access to the same personal power that any successful person has, but only if you have the courage to believe that you do. Claim your personal power and raise your expectations to achieve success. To do that you need to know who you are.

> *"A Negative Mind Will Never*
> *Give You a Positive Life"*
>
> *"The Happiness of Your Life Depends Upon*
> *the Quality of Your Thoughts."*
>
> —Marcus Aurelius

What is YOUR Mindset? Do you know?

To develop a mindset for success you need to know your current mindset. What are your beliefs, values, fears, and assumptions and are these preventing you from being successful? Many people are not ready to be honest with themselves and accept that some of their own beliefs and fears may be keeping them from becoming the best version of themselves.

Go ahead, take a moment and think about your mindset. Ask yourself if you feel responsible for your destiny, or if you tend to make excuses for your current situation. Think about your mindset, particularly when trying to accomplish something that you really want. Do you give up easily? Do you have a plan?

I'm sure you have heard phrases such as "you are what you think" or "you are what you eat" or "if you think you CAN, you are right; if you think you CANNOT, you are also right."

The way you think, your mindset, will make you put forth the effort needed to achieve desired results or not. Whether you will work hard and persist until you achieve your goals or you'll give up after a first try, is based on your mindset. If you think you cannot, then most likely you will give up too soon. You will think that you are not smart enough or that you do not deserve to be happy and successful. Sometimes these feelings are not obvious to you. You may need to do some soul searching in order to identify your true mindset. Carol Dweck's book, Mindset[16] is a great resource as there are many others. I own it and read it several times and I am certain you'll find it useful too.

Take a moment to look at the chart below. On the left is a list of traits or qualities that a person with a fixed mindset may have. On the right, is a list of traits or qualities a person with a growth mindset may have.

Determine which phrase best fits you, and place a checkmark (✓) next to it. Tally it up at the end to see how you score and then define your mindset.

Fixed Mindset		Growth Mindset
I avoid taking risks.	*Or*	I embrace challenges.
I tend to give up easily.	*Or*	I show persistence.
I believe intelligence is fixed at birth.	*Or*	I believe intelligence is constantly developing.
I am often intimidated by others' success.	*Or*	I am inspired by others' success.
I often say, "I can't do this."	*Or*	I say, "I have to work harder."
I avoid new things.	*Or*	I actively seek new opportunities.
I doubt that it is possible to fulfill my dreams.	*Or*	I know I can succeed.
Total		
Your Mindset is _____		

The everyday learner symbolizes a *Growth Mindset*.

"In a Growth Mindset, people understand that their talents and abilities can be developed through effort and persistence. They don't necessarily think everyone's the same or anyone can be Einstein, but they believe everyone can get smarter if they work at it."

The everyday expert symbolizes a *Fixed Mindset*.

> *"In a Fixed Mindset people believe their basic abilities,*
> *their intelligence, their talents, are fixed traits. They have*
> *a certain amount and that's that, and then their goal*
> *becomes to look smart all the time and never look dumb."*

—CAROL DWECK
MINDSET

How did you do? Did most of your answers line up with a growth or a fixed mindset? There is no need to worry if the majority of your answers fell into the 'fixed mindset' category, as long as you decide it is time to take action and to change. You become empowered by first acknowledging the problem and then finding a solution for it.

Do you know someone who has a fixed mindset? Someone who accepts their situation as unchangeable and hopeless? You can see why people in this category are the way they are. They do not believe they can have control over their lives. They may not realize that they can change their thinking and it will change their life.

Do you know someone who has a growth mindset? Is there someone in your close circle whose goal is to go out there and make mistakes, learn from them and become their best selves in the process? Someone who is not afraid to ask questions, who is determined to push themselves and convinced that they can accomplish their goals?

It has been my experience that when your goal is to become the best you can be, then your worries about what others think of you diminishes with time as you become stronger and your belief in your own abilities becomes firmer. In fact, you will be kind and tolerant to your critics because you understand why they behave the way they do – they most likely have a fixed mindset and low self-esteem. Often, it is a reflection of who they are and not of who you are. So, do not spend time or energy on these people. Move on.

> *"Whatever the mind can conceive and believe,*
> *it can achieve."*
>
> —NAPOLEON HILL

Golden Rules of Empowerment

You Cannot Control Everything

It is important to realize that as soon as we give up controlling that which we cannot control, we become free and empowered. We can control how we react to things that happen to us but we cannot control other people. Let's focus our energy and time on things we CAN control – ourselves.

So rather than trying to have control over everything that happens to you, focus on controlling your reaction. For example, if an important meeting was canceled unexpectedly, think of something else you can do with that time that will be productive towards your end goal. Look for the positive in every situation. If you did not get the job you interviewed for, do not agonize over it. Instead, work on improving your resume and your self-confidence skills. Look at the positive side. Perhaps the practice of the job interview itself provided some lessons. Did you get a low grade in your last research paper? That is ok, discuss the results with your professor and ask how to improve your grade next time? Are you angry because you are stuck in traffic? Don't be; you cannot control traffic, so turn on your player and listen to an audio book on self-improvement instead. Always look for the positive in every situation. Something can be learned from any experience. Challenge yourself to find the lessons, even in situations that turn out differently from what you expected.

Be Resilient Against Negative Thinking

There will be times where you doubt yourself. You think "I can't do this," or "I'm not worthy." Do not let negative thoughts hinder your progress. When you face times of self-doubt, ask yourself why you started in the first place as well as what you want to accomplish. Then, you will realize that everything will be worth it in the end. Do not allow yourself to get discouraged along the way. Stay positive and remember to celebrate the small victories so that the downfalls do not seem as deep when they come. Remember that there is no success without failure or lessons as I call them. Embrace your failures or lessons as they teach you better ways to live your life.

Learn to Say No, and Mean It

Do not overwhelm yourself by trying to do too much at once; focus on one goal at a time. The same concept applies to all aspects of your life, not just your aspirations. Let us say, for example, that a close relative of yours asks you for a favor. If doing so would interfere with your own personal goals, it is better for you if you say no. It's not selfish to prioritize yourself ahead of others. You are the one that has to live your life, so you need to make sure you spend your time doing the things that make you happy. Always remember, an empowered woman sometimes needs to say no and she can say no without feeling guilty.

Exercise – Conquer the Mind

To become resilient, empowered, and in control of your own life complete this exercise in your journal.

1 Name a specific goal

2 Visualize your goal

3 Be aware of any negative thoughts about failure and eliminate them

4 How will you show confidence and perseverance until you achieve your goal

5 Share your goal with your friends and family

6 Use the S.M.A.R.T. formula to accomplish your goal

7 Celebrate achieving the goal

8 Plan your next goal

Coaching Moment

Successful people experience countless setbacks during their lifetime. However, their ability to react positively to these obstacles has allowed them to persevere. Do not be afraid of making mistakes; it is part of your long-term success. You know that you deserve a better life; you just have to be willing to **do** something about it.

We examined the difference between a fixed mindset, someone who generally does not believe they can change, and a growth mindset, someone who is willing to put forth the effort to make a change and grow. The exercise provided in this chapter allowed you to determine whether you have a fixed or growth mindset. If you found that you have a fixed mindset, then you also learned what to do to change it. Finally, we discussed some rules of empowerment, and that nothing is impossible to achieve once we set our mind to it.

Emotional Empowerment

"Tough times never last, but tough people do."

—Robert H. Schuller

We often hear stories about people achieving extraordinary things and that they are unique, talented, rich and smart. The truth, however, is much simpler. The people who accomplish extraordinary things are those who are in control of their emotions. You probably know at least one person who seems to be in control of their life. Does it mean that their life is always perfect? No, you and I know that is not the case.

Why is it that some people manage their lives under pressure better than others do? For instance, instead of getting angry when things do not turn out as expected, they remain calm, analyze the situation and then plan their next steps. They are aware of their emotions, and they express themselves effectively. These people have high emotional intelligence (EI), which means they are in control of their emotions.

Did you know that EI is more important than IQ? Yes, it is. That is because it affects our personal and professional relationships, our career, health, and happiness. It rules your life so why not spend the time to understand your emotions. Understand what makes you happy and then do more of it. The same goes for the opposite. Find out what makes you sad or depressed, and do less of it. Let us begin to understand the steps you can take now to improve your EI and get control of your life.

What is Emotional Intelligence?

> *"Painful as it may be, a significant emotional event*
> *can be the catalyst for choosing a direction*
> *that serves us more effectively. Look for the learning."*

—LOUISA MAY ALCOTT

It is the secret to your success in life and business.

Emotional intelligence (EI)[17] is the ability to manage your emotions and understand other people's emotions. People with high EI take risks, know and live in harmony with their values, are action oriented, knowledgeable, and get things done. They embrace challenges and adversity and learn from them without losing power over their emotions. Think about it, everything we do is related to other people, and our emotions often guide our decision-making process and how we feel.

Daniel Goleman wrote a book titled *"Emotional Intelligence – Why It Can Matter More Than IQ" (1995)*[18] and outlined five areas central to EI, which are self-awareness, self-regulation, social skill, empathy, and motivation. Let's examine his model to understand further, what the characteristics of highly emotionally intelligent people have and how you can learn them for yourself.

Self-Awareness

Self-awareness means understanding your emotions and why they drive you to do the things that you do. You no longer let your emotions determine your actions, because you are in control of them. Furthermore, it means that you do not let others deter you from your goals. To become more self-aware, try the following:

Take notes of your feeling and emotions. When you are in a high-stress situation or you suddenly feel any other negative emotion, take note of how you feel. Then, think about what triggered your emotions in the first place. Once you know why you felt the way you do, you can resolve to make changes. Become aware of your emotions and your reaction to them. We will go into more depth on this in the exercise *"Name Your Emotions"* below.

Determine whether the things you are asked to do prevent you from achieving your goal(s). Ask questions until you understand what and why you need to pursue an action. Be respectful and use diplomacy to ensure a positive result. People around you may feel uncomfortable at times, but you should not worry about what other people say or do. Others may attempt to intimidate and manipulate you either to agree with a decision or to buy something you may not want. Stay firm and focus on your intention to understand the topic of discussion to make an informed decision.

Resist saying yes all the time. Practice saying NO without feeling guilty because people who love and respect you will understand. They should want you to be happy, so if they make unreasonable requests without considering your needs, then they may very well not be your friends.

Self-Regulation

A person with high emotional intelligence uses self-regulation as a tool to dispel negative emotion. They realize that some things are out of their control, and when disaster strikes, they're able to get back on their feet and revise their plan. Here are some ideas to help improve self-regulation:

If someone criticizes you, ask questions and do not immediately react to what they say. First, count to five or take a short break before you respond. Decide whether they have a valid critique and work on it to overcome it or just dismiss it. Again, you have control over how you react to things that happen in your life, whether positive or negative.

Take time out. If a particular task or event is causing issues, dedicate time for yourself to think about your state of mind. Remove yourself from the problematic situation and think about your current emotions: what things you can do to change, and areas you can improve upon. Do not rely on someone else to change your emotions, only you can do that. Take the time you need to become stronger and more in control of your life.

Be responsible for your actions. Since you are the only one that can control what you do, you need to take responsibility for your actions. Self-regulation allows an emotionally intelligent woman to be able to think about the consequences of her actions beforehand so that she can react appropriately.

Social Skills

To improve your social skills, try the following:

Listen more often. Emotionally intelligent women listen more than they talk thereby learning more about the people around them. The best way to improve your listening skills is to sign up for a course in effective communication.

Appeal to others' emotions. Being able to understand others' emotions is a form of social skill. The ability to understand and make others feel better about themselves is a sign of high emotional intelligence.

Empathy

If you have high emotional intelligence, you use empathy as a way to understand those around you. Ultimately, the way you behave and respond to situations depends on your ability to manage your emotions and respond to others. Here are some tips on improving your empathy:

Learn to recognize other's feelings. Once you have completed the exercise on naming your emotions, and you feel that you can do so adequately on your own, you will have the proper tools to start putting yourself in others' positions. When you see a friend or co-worker in a high emotional state, try putting yourself in their position. Look at their situation from their point of view and ask yourself what you would do differently.

Pay attention to body language. Take a moment to watch how people interact with each other: sometimes body language reveals a lot more than words. Noticing how someone carries herself in a conversation from afar allows you to identify those same emotions when you're one-on-one.

Consider how your actions affect others. Before you make a big decision, you must learn to consider those who matter the most to you. Is it possible that your plans will get in the way of someone else's success or happiness? A woman with empathy only wants the best for the people around her. If going through on your plans will negatively affect others, you should reconsider your strategy.

Motivation

Your level of emotional intelligence greatly affects your motivation. Emotionally intelligent women do not let negative emotions get in the way of their achievements. To improve your motivation, try the following:

Do not get caught in a cycle of fear and self-doubt. Instead, focus on the end goal and adapt your skills to it. A truly motivated person will continue to take action and seek out opportunities to push herself forward.

Be optimistic. Always strive to see the good in all situations, especially when it is difficult. Remember that you always have a choice *about what to think and feel.* When times get difficult, remember why you started on your venture in the first place. Then look at how far you have come. You may experience a bump in the road every now and again, but that is a part of life. It is up to you to see the bright side of situations and be grateful for all of the things that are going right.

Take the initiative. The one thing that motivates emotionally intelligent people the most is understanding the fact that your goals won't get accomplished unless you actively work towards them. Do not make excuses for why something isn't being done, instead just buckle down and do it, without complaint. And when things go wrong, reassess your strategy and keep on going. Giving up is never an option.

Exercise – Name Your Emotions

Let us try an exercise to increase your emotional intelligence. First, you have to name your emotions. We all know that the most common answer to the question, *how do you feel, is, fine*. But we also know that's rarely ever the truth. We tend to tell people that we are fine for a wide range of reasons, the most common of which is that we do not know how we feel ourselves, and 'fine' is just the easy answer that does not force us to actually look at our situation.

In your journal, write each word and circle the one word that accurately describes how you feel at this very moment.

Angry – Annoyed – Sad – Relaxed – Bored – Joyful – Content – Excited

Now, answer this, how would you like to be feeling one hour from now? Think about it. Maybe now you are content, and in an hour, you want to feel joyful. What steps would you need to take to get there? You do not have to keep your options limited to the list we have here. Think about how you want to feel. Then, realize that it is possible to change how you feel.

In order to change your feelings, you need to assess why something is eliciting a specific emotional response in you in the first place. Then, ask yourself what you can do differently to either confront the feeling or avoid it if necessary. If you possess the ability to change how you feel, you are emotionally empowered.

For some of us, talking about our emotions is hard. If it is difficult for you, you need to ask yourself why. Emotions are a vital part of life. Growing your emotional intelligence will only make your path to success easier to navigate.

To get over your fear of talking about emotions, take a moment to think about some words you would use to describe your emotions. It helps to break them down into categories such as good feelings, bad feelings, neutral feelings, and loving feelings. Here are a few examples from each to get you started.

Good	Bad	Neutral	Loving
Thankful	Depressed	Good	Kind
Brave	Hateful	In-between	Protective
Curious	Unimportant	Indifferent	Warm
Safe	Helpless	Sleepy	Love
Smart	Sick	Well	Aroused

Write a few of your own words here:

_____

_____

_____

_____

_____

_____

_____

Now, looking at the list above and the words that you wrote down in your journal, how many of those can you define on your own? If you struggle to identify what each word means, or how it would feel to experience the word yourself, you should take the time to learn them. Understanding your emotions and differentiating between similar feelings shows strong emotional empowerment.

Coaching Moment

In this chapter, we discuss the importance of Emotional Intelligence (EI) in empowered people. You now understand that emotional intelligence is the ability to fully understand and manage your emotions under pressure.

I discussed five characteristics that are common in emotionally intelligent people. Those characteristics include self-awareness, which is how you understand your emotions and how they drive you, and self-regulation, or the ability to dispel of negative emotion. I also talk about social skills in relation to emotional intelligence such as listening more often and appealing to others' emotions. You now know that empathy is a key requirement when looking to grow your social skills, and motivation includes being optimistic as well as taking the initiative.

Health Empowerment

"If the body be feeble, the mind will not be strong."

—Thomas Jefferson

The truth is that we have to learn how to care for our bodies if we want to be happy and satisfied. I do not want you to spend your hard-earned money on diet schemes. Instead, I want you to educate yourself on how to get your body healthy and happy for life the right way. Instead of making other people rich who are trying to sell you fast and cheap ways to get fit and products that do not work, choose to empower yourself with the knowledge you need to get healthy. Only then will you be in control of your health and life.

Many factors influence your health, such as heredity, the environment, health knowledge, health-care, and lifestyle. The factor that you have the most control over is your way of life, which includes your attitudes, choices, habits, and behavior. Figure out what it is that negatively affects your health, and take steps to remove it by replacing it with positive strategies. It is vital that you differentiate between what you can change, and what you cannot. For example, having a genetic disease that puts you in bad health cannot realistically be cured by a change in lifestyle. However, if there are things you can change that may make dealing with the disease easier, focus on that.

How much Do You Value Your Physical Health?

"Physical fitness is not only one of the most important keys to a healthy body; it is the basis of dynamic and creative intellectual activity."

—John F. Kennedy

Before you commit to making any changes, you first need to ask yourself how much you value your physical health. I know that you value your health, but you also have to answer the question of "WHY" you want to get healthy. Then make it a priority. Having realistic expectations means that you are setting goals and making a plan to achieve them. As you make progress, you will adjust your plan. As you know, anything worthwhile takes time, motivation, sacrifice, and commitment. I cannot think of anything more important than your health. Without optimum health, it is difficult to achieve your other goals and be happy.

Working out is not fun sometimes, especially when you are overwhelmed with work, school, and family. Yes, we have all been there. We have all felt overwhelmed by the demands of our daily lives but if we are honest, being "too busy" is just an excuse most of the time. Think about it, working out is as important as sleeping, eating, and breathing. That is how successful people think about their health. They work on getting their mind and body strong, which leads to overall success and prosperity.

"The body achieves what the mind believes."

What do you believe?

Do you believe you deserve to be healthy and happy?

I know you said yes. You have to choose yourself first just like the mother in a plane who needs to put the mask on first in order to save her child. Being healthy means being happy. Being healthy and happy means being empowered.

Good health requires healthy habits. Not only will you feel amazing, but also your clothes will fit better, your self-esteem and confidence will increase, and you will live a longer, happier and healthier life. That is your ultimate goal, to be happy and in control of every aspect of your life – to be EMPOWERED. And to be a role model for those you love.

It's never too late to get healthy. Age is just a number.

Start today. Start right this minute. Are you ready?

It is imperative that you design a plan that works for your schedule and disposition. For most people, it is best to work out first thing in the morning. However, if that is not possible, then any time is a good time. Be flexible and try different times and exercises before you set an exercise routine. Regardless, make sure that you commit to moving and challenging your body every day.

You deserve to be healthy and happy, and only you can make that happen.

Exercise – Reasons to get Healthy

In your journal, write your reasons for getting healthy. Set a timer for 5 minutes and write down all the reasons that come to mind as to why you want to begin to work out and get healthy. Be sure the reasons are compelling and realistic so that they will motivate you when life gets in the way.

A Strong Mind Requires a Strong and Healthy Body

"Health is not a condition of matter, but of mind."

—MARY BAKER EDDY

Whether you are starting a new exercise routine today or you have been working out for a while, what matters is that you are making progress in the right direction and maintaining consistency. Yes, consistency is key to making progress and achieving desired results.

First, prioritize your workout time, and ensure it is on your schedule. At this point, you are concerned with creating a healthy habit by working out at least three to five times a week. Again, pick a time that works for you and fits into your lifestyle. For me, I prefer to work out in the morning. However, when that is not possible, I make sure to get it done at some point during the day. In fact, there are plenty of benefits to working out first thing in the morning – more energy, lower stress levels throughout the day, greater productivity and clarity of goals, better disposition, and control over things that happen during the day. In one word –you will feel empowered. Being energized by a morning workout puts you in control of how you react to the things that happen during the day.

Second, start moving and get active. Be sure to vary your workout routine, so your body will be challenged enough and will not get "bored" or stagnant. You should always challenge your body and push through your comfort zone to achieve great results. After all, you cannot do the same routine every day and expect your results to continuously improve. Change is good. Remember, working out should be fun so find activities that you enjoy doing and do them intentionally. Choose from walking, biking, running, playing sports, weight training, and any other activities you like. Be sure to always have an extra pair of walking shoes in the car, so you will not have an excuse for not working out. For example, I get bored easily, so I vary my exercise routine all the time. I also like to push myself and improve my workout exercise so that I can achieve more with less time.

Third, find someone to work out with and be accountable to each other. Call up your girlfriends, propose getting fit together, and use each other as a support system. Or look up walking groups in your area and sign up. Who knows, you may even make some new friends who, like yourself, are on their way to empowerment. Go even a step further and tell everyone you know about this book and organize a meeting to discuss the book and the ways to reach empowerment.

Last, be committed to and consistent with your workout schedule. If you feel like not working out one day, do not stress too much about it. It happens. The secret is not giving up. Take the time you need and then get back to your workout routine.

My Morning Routine

*"The secret to your success and happiness
is hidden in your daily routine"*

An empowered morning routine provides you with a sense of purpose and direction, which connects to your understanding of your mental, physical, spiritual and emotional levels. I try to live every day with purpose and intention. I know exactly what it is that I want to focus on and achieve each day. To make sure it happens I create S.M.A.R.T. goals and a plan to achieve them. At the end of each day I reflect asking myself questions such as,

What did I accomplish today?

What did I learn?

Was my plan successful? Do I need adjustments?

What actions can I take to have a better tomorrow?

What knowledge do I need to perform better tomorrow?

These questions help me be aware, responsible and accountable for what happens in my daily life. When it comes to my workout routine, I use the same formula. I set S.M.A.R.T. goals, come up with a plan of action, adjust and reflect as I improve each day to ensure constant growth.

"A goal without a plan is just a wish"

Having a morning routine means that I dedicate time every morning to specific activities that are imperative to my success and overall well-being. You cannot become an empowered woman without knowing what the day holds for you. So what kind of a day you would like to have? What do you want to achieve today or tomorrow? These questions help you come up with your plan for the day, and a morning routine will help you set the day so that you achieve the things planned. It is important to remember that adopting new, successful habits will not change your life overnight. However, persistence and consistency are key to achieving results.

Your morning routine may look different from mine; however, most of my morning activities are similar to the successful and empowered people everywhere. The goal is to develop your own morning routine that works for you and helps you to become empowered and successful. Don't be afraid to try different activities and see how you feel.

Now I am ready to introduce you to my own empowering morning routine, which includes these activities:

Wakeup	6:00 am
Meditation	6:00 am
Visualization	6:15 am
Affirmation	6:20 am
Workout	6:45 – 7:45 am
Breakfast	7:50 am
Reading	8:00 – 8:45 am
Ready to begin a productive day by 9:00 am	

Let us discuss briefly my morning routine and help you develop your own morning routine today.

Wake up – at 6 am, which means that I have to be in bed by 11 pm at the latest. It is important to get sufficient sleep and like it or not, it is true that most successful people wake up early.

Meditation – I meditate for at least 5 minutes, sometimes up to 20 minutes. I usually meditate several times a day. Meditation is very common these days and people from all walks of life use meditation to clear the mind, stay calm, for better sleep, to reduce stress, increase awareness, and mindfulness.

Visualization – I visualize for two or three minutes my day, my goals, obstacles I may have, a situation I may be in and how I should behave to ensure progress towards achieving my goals. It is important to be realistic that achieving success is not a straight-line journey. You will have difficulties and how you overcome them will determine whether you will achieve your goals or not. For example, visualizing the empowered woman you will become will allow you to make choices that will lead you to achieve your goals. Or staying calm while in traffic is the right thing to do; after all, you do not have control over the traffic situation so why become upset? Use those minutes for positive visualization.

Affirmation –I use affirmations on a daily basis throughout the day not only in the morning. I have books on affirmation, and many favorite ones are on my walls around the house, on my computer screen, and in my head, of course. Positive affirmation raises awareness, especially when you think negatively about yourself without knowing. They work to shift your negative thinking into a positive one. You can start with a few and write them down, or print your favorite ones as I did and have them displayed in the kitchen, bathroom, bedroom and read them aloud until they become part of your thinking habit. You could even have a few in your purse or your car, so if you find yourself thinking negatively or stressed out, you'll shift your thinking to your favorite positive affirmation.

Here are some of my favorite affirmations, which you may also use:

✓ Today is going to be an amazing day because I choose to make it so.

✓ I am grateful for everything and everyone in my life, and I make it my business to let them know.

✓ Today is great. Tomorrow is going to be greater.

✓ I use my mind and thoughts to create opportunities for myself and enhance my life.

✓ I deserve to be rich and empowering because I add value to other people's lives.

✓ I have the ability to visualize every aspect of my success.

✓ I view all my experiences as opportunities to learn and grow.

✓ Every day, in every way, I am getting better and better.

✓ I am only attracted to food that serves my highest good.

✓ I am perfectly healthy, mentally and physically, and I do all the things I need to maintain my health.

✓ I give myself some quiet time every day. It is important that I connect with my deeper self.

✓ I am my best friend. Other friends come and go, but I am always here for me.

✓ I respect my boundaries and myself. I insist that others respect them, too.

Work out – I work out consistently 4-5 times a week, usually early in the morning. Notice I said consistently, which is an important factor in maintaining your weight and overall health. My workout includes cardio, weight and stretching. I usually jog or brisk walk 3-4 miles followed by 15 – 20 minutes of weights and finish up with plank and stretching. I also vary my workout routine, so I do not get bored, and after a while, my body does not like it either so I will do cross training, yoga or ride my bike. I will share a secret with you – did you know that if you exercise first thing in the morning on an empty stomach, your body will use stored fat for energy because you have no food or glycogen to give you the energy to exercise? Another benefit of exercising in the morning is that you will not have to worry about it later, won't have to shower again and change clothes, and also you make sure it gets done. If you cannot do it in the morning, it's fine, just do it whenever it fits your schedule. After all, it is a lifetime activity so it must work with your schedule.

Breakfast – Breakfast is a very important meal of the day, and it becomes even more important after a workout. Do not skip breakfast. I prepare my meals in advance so that I always have something healthy to eat when needed.

Read – I read every morning and every evening. Reading is an active mental process as it engages the brain, which needs exercises to keep it strong and healthy. I rarely watch television and when I do, it is a movie or documentary.

Ready to begin my work day – My morning routine is complete, and now I am enthusiastic and ready to begin my working day. I know it will be productive because I have planned it. My morning routine inspires and motivates me to do the best each day and never to forget that tomorrow we have another opportunity to do it better. Therefore, having a morning routine and taking care of your mind, body and soul is a fundamental part of your journey toward empowerment and success. Don't take it for granted. Take care of your health today and every day. You deserve it.

Feed the Body and Brain Well

"The spirit is the life,
the mind is the builder
and the body the result."

—EDGAR CAYCE

Did you know that what you eat affects how you think?

I frequently watch PBS, the Public Broadcasting Service, and one of their successful health programs is Dr. Daniel Amen's[19], a well – renowned American psychiatrist, a brain disorder specialist, and director of the Amen Clinics, which talks about the importance of taking care of our brain. Your brain matters and we should learn how to care for it. We cannot separate the body from the brain because they rely on each other. If the brain is strong and healthy, the body is most likely also strong and healthy.

How you feel, think, behave, react, and treat others reflects how your brain feels. If it feels good, you will most likely feel good as well, which means you are feeding it proper nutrition, getting enough sleep and keeping it healthy.

A fit and healthy body says a lot about who you are as a person. You know that people "evaluate" you based on what they see. Your appearance reflects your work ethics, self-discipline, determination, self-respect and how empowered you are in your life. You may or may not be aware that we make a first impression within seven seconds of meeting someone. Therefore, the way you look could send a strong signal about who you are and how you feel

94

about yourself. You want to work out, eat well and look great. You deserve to be healthy and happy. *You only have 1 chance and seven seconds to make a great first impression.*

After all, what is the point of making money and working hard if you do not have the physical health to be able to enjoy it? The better your physical condition, the more energy, and motivation you will have to carry on productive work. Let's be honest – we feel empowered when we feel and look good.

Become Healthy Empowered

Begin your journey to being empowered in your health by setting a clear and specific goal. You must believe that you will achieve it because if you don't, then you will sabotage your effort. Visualize your new healthy self. How would you feel and look? Remain consistent regardless what life gives you and always remember that it is up to you to persist and achieve what you desire.

Exercise – Setting Smart Goals

I just wanted to remind you that once you begin your exercise routine, you will undergo extraordinary changes. It may be hard to imagine if you are just starting out, but trust me on this as I am telling you from experience. I will share more about this with you later in the book. By taking good care of your health, you will look and feel amazing, which makes you more confident and empowered.

Be ready for a new you, the empowered woman that is already within you.

You are already familiar with the S.M.A.R.T goal formula. We will discuss in depth how the S.M.A.R.T. goal setting works, later in the book. For now, take a note of it and be sure to use it for every goal you set for yourself. It never disappoints.

S.M.A.R.T. goal-setting formula example:

✓ Specific

I want to lose 10 pounds

✓ Measurable

Measure your progress often. Whatever you can measure, you can manage.

✓ Attainable

Set yourself up for success. Goal must be attainable. You need a challenge but do not make it too big that you cannot reach it.

✓ Relevant

Make sure YOU want to do it. Do it for YOU not anyone else.

✓ Time-bound

Must have a deadline. I will lose 10 pounds in three months (3.3 a month).

Coaching Moment

I don't know why so many people spend their money on diets and programs that do not work. Do you want to keep spending hundreds of dollars on diets that do not work? If your answer is negative which I hope it is then you are ready to implement a workout plan that will change your life forever. Start by scheduling time to exercise, and commit to a routine. Find someone to work out with and be accountable to each other. Always use the S.M.A.R.T. goal setting formula to set yourself up for success. Eat nutritional food, plan your meals in advance, always have healthy snacks in the house and do not buy anything that is not good for you. On my website, you will find free resources about my S.M.A.R.T. Goals and how I lost 10 pounds in three months, and much more. Go to: *www.valmargarit.com* for more.

Financial Empowerment

"Thought is the original source of all wealth,
all success, all material gain, all great
discoveries and inventions, and all achievement."

—Claude M. Bristol

I didn't have a lot of money growing up but we were healthy and happy. I never thought I was poor because everyone in the village lived in pretty much the same way. When you live on a farm, you eat what you grow, so I worked alongside my parents after school and summer breaks, growing vegetables, raising chickens, pigs and cows, and tobacco. That was hard work, but that was our life. That was our reality. Of course, I wanted to have more money but that was not possible at the time. Therefore, when I was ready to leave I was also ready to learn how to make money. I wanted to make my own money and become financially independent. In fact, I do not think we can ever be free without financial independence, especially for women.

Don't you agree?

I learned that to become financially independent is a choice. It is a state of mind. Once you understand that you deserve to be financially successful, you begin to change your mindset about money, how you make it and how you spend it. In the beginning, I didn't know much about managing money. I thought that if I went to school, educated myself and got a higher degree, then I would get a job, earn a salary and live happily ever after. I was wrong. Making money has nothing to do with being financially independent, as you probably know. No matter how much money we make, it never seems to be enough.

That is not how financially successful people think. After all, making money is a skill just like any other. Therefore, I began reading about financially successful people and their strategies. I read finance books by Tom Stanley, Suze Orman, David Bach, Napoleon Hill, Tony Robbins and many others, listened to podcasts and audiobooks and used that knowledge over and over again in my own life. I realized that earning a college degree or the amount of money I make a month had nothing to do with becoming financially independent. What I needed was to become financially literate; to learn HOW to manage, invest, spend, and save my money.

I learned that you cannot be happy unless you are financially independent. After all, even people who have a good income aren't necessarily financially independent or happy. There is more to it than that. There is this fear most women have about asking for more money at work, talking about money and making financial decisions. Let's face it; schools don't teach people how to live a good life: how to be happy, how to value money, and how to invest it. We have to figure it out on our own, the hard way. And as a woman, it is even more complicated and urgent that we address it because we make less money to begin with. However, you can change that in your favor by empowering yourself with the knowledge you need to use in order to become financially literate and independent.

Do not be afraid. Remember, KNOWLEDGE IS POWER IF WE KNOW HOW TO USE IT. Take a look at the following facts before we discuss practical strategies to manage your finances. Again, do not be afraid. Stay with me, keep an open mind and be ready to take the first steps toward financial empowerment.

Empowered Women Have A Budget

"The wealth of the rich can be stolen or burnt, but the happiness and the wisdom of the wise remains."

—Unknown

To become financially independent, pay off debts, and save money, you need a budget. There is no other way. A budget includes your monthly income from all of your sources, your needs after taxes, your wants, and allocating money to each area of your life. There are many online resources to manage finances. I use mint.com for managing my finances. I create budgets, monitor my expenses, debts, savings, and investments, receive personalized alerts, and schedule automatic bill payments, so I'll never be late and pay late fees. In short, I am in control of managing my finances in one place. I know exactly where I stand financially and that's very empowering. I want you to do the same. Go to *www.mint.com*[20]

and sign up for an account (did I tell you it is FREE?). There you'll find information on how to set it up, how to create budgets and everything else you need. You'll feel amazing once you get it done.

Alternatively, if you prefer to write down your budget, or use planners, you can do that as well. Budgets are typically drawn out on a month-to-month basis, so the first thing you will need to do is write down all the income you make in a one-month period.

Use the form on the left to write down all of your income for the next full monthly period. The chart on the right is an example of how yours could look.

Date	Source	Amount		Date	Source	Amount
				Oct 6	Full-Time	672.14
				Oct 13	Full-Time	598.43
				Oct 20	Full-Time	646.82
				Oct 27	Full-Time	713.48
Total				Total		2,630.87

Once you know how much money you're bringing in, you need to take a look at the money that goes out. First, write down all of your expected monthly expenses. Then, make sure you leave enough room for other expenses such as gas and grocery. Use the form on the left to write down all of your expenses for the next full monthly period. The chart on the right is an example of how yours could look.

Date	Item	Amount
Total		

Date	Item	Amount
Oct 1	Rent	540.00
Oct 9	Electric/Gas	137.49
Oct 12	Water	112.17
Oct 14	Car Insur	83.42
Oct 19	Phone	48.79
Oct 22	Credit Card	25.00
Oct 1	Gas	35.00
Oct 15	Gas	35.00
Oct 1	Grocery	75.00
Oct 7	Grocery	75.00
Oct 14	Grocery	75.00
Oct 21	Grocery	75.00
Oct 27	Grocery	75.00
Misc	Misc	150.00
Total		1,541.87

The goal is that your total expenses will be less than your income. If not, take the time to see where you can start cutting expenses. We go into further detail on this in the following section, "Stay in Control of Your Money."

Empowered Women Pay Off Debts

"Never spend your money before you have it."

—THOMAS JEFFERSON

I know exactly how it feels to have credit card debt. It doesn't feel good to know that we owe more than we own. The relationship we have with money is an emotional one and money can make us feel either worth it or worthless. When we feel worth it, we are in control. We are happy and empowered to make sound financial decisions. On the other hand, when we feel worthless we feel less confident or motivated to take care of our finances and we go out and spend more. In fact, there is a correlation between the way we feel and see ourselves, whether we are happy, confident, strong, motivated and the degree to which we are in control of our finances.

You have the power to reset the finance button and begin living an honest life. No more debts, or pretending to be someone you are not, buying stuff you cannot afford, and giving away your hard-earned money to marketers who try to sell you things you do not need. No, you deserve better. You need to turn your fear into action. You cannot afford to live paycheck to paycheck, pay the minimum on your credit cards and just watch your life go by. Getting out of debt is the most important action you can take to become financially and emotionally empowered.

Call your highest-interest-rate credit card banks and simply ask them to lower your interest rate. Then, if you have not done so already, go to your finance management software, *www.mint.com*

and create an account for each credit card. Allocate a monthly payment for each account. That's it. Mint will calculate and give you a visual of how much you owe and when you will be able to pay it off based on your allocated monthly payment. You have to make sure to use only your debit card for expenses. Cut up all of your credit cards and only keep the one with the lowest interest rate and use it only for emergencies.

Another method is debt consolidation, especially if you have a lot of credit card debt and cannot handle it on your own. A debt management company will call your creditors on your behalf and negotiate for a lower interest rate. The debt management company takes on all of your debt, and you only pay one monthly payment to them. Of course, there is a fee for this service. But it may be the right thing for you, depending on your circumstances.

If it's not possible to lower your interest rate on a credit line, or hiring a debt management company to consolidate your debt isn't for you, you could try using the debt snowball method. This strategy is extremely useful if you have more than one debt, such as multiple credit cards, mortgage, or other loans. Using this method, you will start with the account with the smallest balance first, paying more than the minimum balance. You can pay $50, $100, or even $500 more than the minimum balance, whatever you can afford, while your other debts remain at the minimum balance. Soon, you'll have one less account, and you can start using what you would have been paying towards that, to the next smallest balance, and so on until you're out of debt. This method can sometimes take a couple of years or more if you have a lot of credit lines, but it is well worth it in the end when you are debt-free and feeling empowered.

Not All Debt is Bad

Student loan debts can be considered a good debt because it enables you to pursue your dreams that otherwise wouldn't have been possible. I have student loans, and I am paying them. I am proud to have been able to achieve my dreams by earning an education that I partly paid with loans. Of course, you need to be careful and borrow only the amount you need to pay for your education.

A mortgage is also good debt, assuming it is within your means. I know people who live in houses they cannot afford and have to work extra hours or a second job to pay the mortgage. Why would anyone do that? You, the empowered woman, understand that the cost of your home should be below your means so that more money goes into your saving and investing accounts, not to the mortgage lender. I bought a condominium that is below my means, and my mortgage is less than what I spent when I was renting. When I was shopping for a condominium, my realtor would send me listings of condominiums that were above my budget. After all, realtors make commission based on sales, so it is in their interests to sell high priced properties. I told the realtor that I only expected to be notified of properties within my budget and in my desired areas. It's up to you to always think about what is best for you and your finances. Stay within your budget, and always try to purchase only the things you need.

Medical expenses and taking care of your parents are also good debts. My mom lived with me for several winters, from October to March. I had a small one-bedroom apartment that I shared with her. I was responsible for her and all of her expenses including round-trip international flights. In fact, several times I had to fly to Europe-London, Frankfurt, or Paris, to pick her up because she had difficulties connecting to the US bound flight. She didn't speak English, saw the airport as big and confusing and she was getting older and needed help. I was a graduate student at the time, working several jobs to care for both of us. I had to use credit cards for some of my expenses, and I am glad I did because it allowed me to care for my mom and to have her in my life and enjoy time together. I knew I could pay it back but my mom was here for a while, and there was no guarantee that she would be back. In fact, she died four years ago, just three months after she left her "Florida winter residence." Imagine how I felt knowing that I did everything I could for her. Even now as I write this, there are tears streaming down my face.

The point here is that there are certain expenses in your life, which benefit you more than they cause harm. You just need to find the balance and only incur expenses that add to your overall happiness and that of the people you love. Now that we have agreed that not all debt is bad, let's take a look at the expenses that are harming your financial empowerment.

Stay in Control of Your Money

"Do not let others set the standard about how much money you should have, or about what you should do with it, for you are the only one who could ever accurately define that."

—ABRAHAM – HICKS

We work very hard, at least 40 hours a week, we get paid every two weeks or monthly and then what do we do? We go shopping. We sometimes spend our hard-earned money on things we do not need to impress people who may not care. We live in a consumer-based society that makes it very easy to buy today on credit and pay later. Often by the time we pay off a large purchase, we learn that it cost us double or more, depending on how fast we paid back the initial purchase. Most people carry debt at high-interest rates, they do not have savings, and they live paycheck to paycheck. That's not the way to live your life if you want to become financially independent.

You need to have an honest relationship with your money where every dime, dollar, and financial choice counts. You need to learn the difference between needs and wants. A need is something necessary to survive like food, shelter, clothes, and a car if you need to drive to work. A want is everything else such as extra clothes you don't need and probably don't wear, extra shoes, purses, jewelry, extra TV channels, eating out instead of cooking at home, and other services you may want but do not need. These things are not necessary, and therefore you CAN live without them.

Now is a good time to be honest, take a deep breath and take inventory of your spending and shopping habits, look carefully at your NEEDS and WANTS and find out where you can cut expenses, so you stop giving your money away and begin saving it for yourself.

Here are some examples that I use in my own life and could be helpful for you to start saving money:

Your Coffee

Do you drink coffee? Do you make it at home or buy it outside? I make my own coffee at home and seldom buy it outside unless I am traveling.

Did you know that one medium-size Starbucks coffee a day costs you $2.85, which means you are spending $1,040.25 a year on morning coffee? That's just coffee. You can invest that money or use it to pay off debts or put into a retirement account. You do not need to be a professional financial planner to figure this much out. Of course, you can always hire one. But for now, you have everything you need in this book to get control over your finances; cut down your expenses, create a budget, and pay off debt. You just need to ACT. Without ACTION, nothing ever happens. Don't you agree?

The same goes for that fancy wine or premium beer or tea. How much are they costing you per week or per year? Take a good look at these "little" expenditures and decide to be more responsible with your money.

Be Careful of What You Watch On TV

Do not watch shopping or food channels on which they use appealing marketing techniques make you buy things you don't need. If you don't watch it, you won't buy it. Every time you turn on the TV, someone is trying to sell you something, or tell you that something is wrong with you and you need to buy their products to improve yourself and feel better. Let me tell you, *there is nothing wrong with you, and you are perfect the way you are.* You are a beautiful, strong, and confident woman. If there is anything you want to change for the better, you can do it yourself at a fraction of the cost or even free. It will be your informed decision. So, stop spending money on what you don't need. Advertising is inviting (it is what supports television broadcasting) and it is designed to seduce you into spending your money.

Quit Spending Money Shopping Online

Close your Amazon.com account if you have one. Do you need it? Why? Ask the question – can you live without it? Most likely, the answer is yes, in which case you'll save a lot of money and time. Why do you think Amazon.com sells "everything" charges a yearly fee of $99 and offers free shipping, handling, and sub-scriptions? Nothing is free and you know it. Amazon knows it too, which is why they have this business model in the first place. They know people can be financially irresponsible, shop impulsively, and love instant gratification.

I had an Amazon.com account for one year after I bought my condominium. I knew I would need to make several purchases and wanted to save money and time. And I did. Once the year was over, I closed the account. Now I only buy things that I NEED. I am a conscious shopper.

Phone

Do you have the latest phone model with all the accessories and a comprehensive plan? What is the cost? Do you need it or just want it? I never pay more than $50 a month, and my plan provides more than enough services for me. Can you switch to a cheaper plan? Find out. Most likely, you will find a plan that offers what you need for less than what you pay now.

Unused Subscriptions

Do you pay for every known TV channels but you only use a few? Call your company and negotiate to pay only for what you need and use. The same goes for streaming services. If you are not using that Netflix account, it's time to get rid of it.

Gym Membership

Did you know that 67% of people never use their gym membership[21]? Do you have a gym membership? Are you one of the people who pay a monthly gym membership fee and seldom use it? Most people sign up for a membership at the beginning of the year and use it for a month or so and around mid-February stop going to the gym but continue to pay the monthly fee. Don't do that. That's your hard-earned money, and you deserve to have it and enjoy it, not give it away. For instance, I use a $10 a month local gym membership and use it primarily for weights and strength exercises as I enjoy doing my cardio outdoors. At $10 a month, $120 a year, I know I get my money's worth. Check the options in your area, call the workout facilities, ask questions and then make an informed decision that is within your budget.

Do you have exercise equipment that you haven't used in a while? Well, if you don't use it, get rid of it, sell it or donate it.

Beauty Supplies

Did you know that women spend about $250 a month or $200, 000 in a lifetime on beauty products?[22] How about you? How much do you spend on beauty supplies? As a woman, I understand that we need to feel good and look good. However, I believe that we could do better and save some of that money for ourselves. We are beautiful. Beauty is in the eye of the beholder. It is an inside job. We need to believe that we are beautiful and instead of spending a ton of money on beauty products that we do not need, we should work on our self-confidence and self-esteem. When we feel good about ourselves from inside out, we will not need as many beauty products. I know that society tells us what to do, how to look and feel but we are smart and know that beauty comes from within. Nothing and no one can make you feel beautiful. You have to believe you are beautiful. You are beautiful. I am beautiful.

Groceries

Always groceries shop with a list and only buy what's on it. Likewise, never go to the grocery store hungry because chances are that you will buy things you do not need and that are not very healthy. Buy in bulk, especially if you have a family. Be aware of every item you buy and how much you pay for it. How much do you think you'll save by changing your spending habits? $200, $500 or $1000? That's how you too can become financially empowered by treating money with respect, counting every dollar and being accountable and responsible for yourselves.

Now you are in charge of your finances. Every day you delay means less money in your savings account and more stress. You deserve better, and you are the only one who can take control over your financial life. The good news is that you CAN do it. It just takes awareness, determination, and commitment. If you set a budget, pay down those debts, and control your spending, you will be one step closer to financial empowerment.

Coaching Moment

This chapter is all about financial empowerment. Once you decide that you deserve to be financially empowered, the next step is to change your mindset about money and look at how you spend it. Making money has nothing to do with being financially independent; as we have discussed, there's much more to it than that.

We discussed what it means to be financially empowered, particularly as a woman. We did two different exercises in this chapter, creating a budget and learning how to pay down debts faster, both of which are vital parts of becoming financially independent and empowered. Now you know what it takes to create and maintain a budget, as well as possible ways to get rid of that debt.

While it's generally a good idea not to have debt, that isn't the case 100% of the time. There are instances where creating debt can be a good thing. Some examples shown here include student loans, mortgages, or health-related expenses. These expenses can sometimes greatly benefit your overall happiness more than they can cause harm. You just need to differentiate an unnecessary expense from a valid one.

Finally, we talked about a few areas in your life that you can try to cut down on those unnecessary payments, such as coffee, online spending, your phone, unused subscriptions, gym memberships, beauty supplies, and groceries. Take an honest look at what you are spending and stop wasting money on things you don't need. You will be one step closer to financial empowerment.

Career Empowerment

Do you love your job?

Are you passionate about what you do for a living?

We spend more than a third of our lives working, and most people do not enjoy their work. Research studies show that 80% of people do not enjoy or despise their current job[23]. If you are one of the people who does not love their job, it is time to change that. It is better to try doing something you love and fail than to live your life doing something you hate. To start, go back to the

115

"Who Am I" chapter and review your values, passions, and talents. You may be tempted to say to yourself "I do not have time for it, or that I have bills to pay," all of which are true. However, what you may not know is that you CAN change your career and do work you love.

An empowered woman has control over her career. She always learns and grows, and tries to do work that aligns with her values. Happiness is important to her. This chapter will go over things that you can do to get ahead and feel empowered in the workplace. We will discuss the opportunity to get a raise or a promotion, the gender pay gap issue, and the necessary skills and education for a competitive career. We live in a globalized, information-based, skills focused economy where knowing means growing.

Raises and Promotions

A study conducted by McKinsey & Company and LeanIn[24] shows that women are less likely to receive challenging projects, to have access to senior leaders and to be promoted than men. The report shows that more women than men asked for a raise, but they were told they were being" bossy", aggressive" or "intimidating.

There are several disadvantages women face when asking for a raise or promotion. Women are less likely to receive feedback, even when they request it, and are often seen as pushy or intimidating if they ask more than once. This is not a surprise to you if you are a woman in the workforce. It is common for women not to ask for what they want for fear of seeming too aggressive. That is why when they seek to negotiate their wages or position within a company; they are often met with disappointment.

There are also those who have no desire to pursue a higher position and pay within the company. The main reason for this seems to be the need for balance between work and family life. This could be because women, in general, anticipate a harder path with more obstacles and do not think the cost of sacrificing their quality of life at home outweighs the benefits of advancing their career.

Why Do We Still Have Gender Wage Gap?

Usually it is what you do not know that causes pain and suffering, which is why self-awareness is so important. If you want different results, start doing things differently. Once you do, you will find that what you didn't know may hurt you. Most women are afraid to talk about finances. For example, they are afraid to speak up and negotiate a salary or ask for a raise. Many think that the boss will do it for them. That is not true. If you wait for your boss to give you a raise you may have to wait for a long time. Maybe forever. You are responsible and accountable for your career. Take control of your finances now so that you do not have to worry about money in the future.

You and I know that you deserve equal pay for equal work. I ask that you join me on this journey to financial literacy and empowerment. Like yourself, I am disturbed at the inequality but committed to doing my part to earn what I am worth, and I hope you will stand up for yourself too. My value in the workplace should not be based on my gender. How do you feel about working as hard as the men in your field and being paid 20 percent less just because you are a woman, or 30 percent less if you are a woman of color[25]? In order to achieve change, YOU need to become aware of what you do not know so you can protect yourself and take action toward becoming financially empowered.

Look at the gender pay gap facts. According to the latest research from The American Association of University Women, here are the FACTS you need to know:

The Pay Gap Compared to White Men's Earnings - 2015

	Current Population Survey (CPS)	American Community Survey (ACS)
Hispanic or Latina	**54%**	54%
African American	**63%**	62%
White (non-Hispanic)	**75%**	76%
Asian	**85%**	90%
Native Hawaiian and Other Pacific Islander	--	**60%**
American Indian and Alaska Native	--	**58%**

Sources: U.S. Census Bureau, Current Population Survey, *Annual Social and Economic Supplements*, Table P-38 and U.S. Census Bureau, *2015 American Community Survey 1-Year Estimates*

1   Women earn an average of 80 cents for every dollar men make[26].

2   A woman working full-time earns an average of $10,800 less per year than a man does. This adds up to about half a million over a career life.

3   The gender pay gap varies by state. For instance, as of 2015, the gender income gap was the smallest in New York where full time women are paid 89 percent of what men are paid. Wyoming came in last with the largest gender income gap; women are paid 64 percent of what men are paid. Look up your state and find out how much money you make compared to men.

4   It becomes even more painful if you are a woman of color. Here is the breakdown: When compared to men of their own race women of color are doing better, between 80-85 percent. However, when compared to white men, African-American women earn only 60 percent, Hispanic women earn only 55%, and Asian women earn 84% of what white men make.

5   Women receive less pension dollars than men do. Moreover, because women live longer than men, they also need to have more retirement income to be able to care for themselves.

6   Today, more than 30 percent of women between the ages 65-75 live below the poverty line. Imagine reaching the retirement age and not being able to enjoy life and live well. Imagine being retired and having to go back to work in order to survive. You plan for a more secure future no matter the situation, age, or race, but you have to act now.

The gender pay gap will not be closed for at least 43 years, according to the report. Since we are already losing money by being paid less than men are, it is paramount that not only we learn how to become financially empowered and spend less but also to ensure that we ask for what we are worth. Become financially empowered and in control of your career and finances.

Skills You Need to Succeed in The Workplace

As a woman, you may be undervalued or underpaid or both, in the workplace. However, there are several ways to increase your chance to earn what you deserve and to make career progress. While a college degree is necessary for most jobs, it is not enough anymore.

A college degree alone will not secure a job unless we also become proficient in "people skills," more commonly known as "soft skills". The more you demonstrate these skills, the faster your career will advance and your overall quality of life will improve as well.

1   Effective Communication Skills

How are you going to market yourself and persuade others to hire you? Although a higher education degree is imperative for most jobs, you need to persuade others of the reasons, they should invest in you and that you are the best candidate for the job.

2   Ability to Relate to Others

What type of personality do you have? Are you friendly, well rounded, and worldly? If so, you will not have many obstacles to relating to other people. It shows that you understand and tolerate differences.

3   Empathy

Walk a mile in my shoes and then you will understand me. You've heard of this expression which is at the core of people skills. When you show compassion, you understand other people's motivations, aspirations, and fears. This makes you a great friend, leader, manager or coach.

4   Critical Thinking

Critical thinking skills are a deliberate thought process. You are able to consider multiple perspectives, consequences and use reason and evidence to solve problems. Being informed and suspending judgment while seeking the right solution to a problem are imperative to becoming a critical thinker.

5   Flexibility and Adaptability

A good people person is flexible and adaptable. You need to be able to understand people's behavior to be able to respond to a situation that requires you to make adjustments. You have to be able to roll with the punches when necessary.

6   Persuasion

Lacking persuasion skills is not an option. You need to be able to convey your idea or make a strong argument for a cause or an idea you want to promote. You need to persuade others why you or your idea is the "the best" product.

7   Negotiation

Negotiation skills are imperative in the workplace and life. There are always options when it comes to sales and buying, or negotiating your salary. You need to know to negotiate to ensure you get the best value for your money or achieve the best outcome from your efforts.

8   Curiosity – Being Open Minded

Keep an open mind, and you will always learn and grow. People also love to work with "learners" who are curious about the world around them and know that no one has all the answers.

9   Body Language

It is necessary that you are aware of your body language as often we are judged not by what we say but by what our body language conveys – from gestures, expressions, appearance, and tone. Recall I said that we only have about seven seconds to make a first impression?[27] Much of the impression we give is based on nonverbal cues.

10 Leadership Skills

You are a leader for yourself and those around you. Lead by example, and you'll be far more successful in your workplace and life.

11 Motivate and Support Others

Believe in yourself and others. Support, encourage and inspire others to do and be their best. Make a difference and live each day with awareness and intention.

Live your life by design NOT by chance.

Top Ten Women's Career Empowerment Qualities

"Welcome to planet Earth. There is nothing
that you cannot be or do or have, and your work here,
your lifetime career, is to seek joy."

—ABRAHAM – HICKS

1 Believe

As an empowered woman, you must believe that you are capable of pursuing your dreams and living a happy life. If you do not believe it, no one will. This is because having faith in yourself helps you have less fear as well as take more calculated risks. You will do this because you know that every experience, good or bad, is one step closer to attaining your goal. You are persistent and resilient, and you know that success takes time, hard work, and sacrifice.

2 You Have Choices

Empowerment is about learning that there are choices in life. No one can decide for you. You must decide what you want to do and what will make you happy. You have already done so in this book, through the getting-to-know-yourself exercises. The next step is to make your choices and figure out how to get what you want.

If you limit yourself to what you think people expect of you, you take away your ability to choose for yourself. This is especially important when considering career paths. Make your own decisions and plan for yourself if you want to be happy and feel empowered.

3 Find YOUR Balance

We often hear about having a work/life balance. I believe we need to choose work that we love which will make us happy. Doing so will give us balance in life. When we love what we do and surround ourselves with good, caring people then our values and desires are in alignment.

4   Have a Powerful Network

It is imperative that you develop a network of positive people on which you can depend. You must choose to utilize the benefits available from the people in your life by asking for help when you need it. They are the people that support your goals and are willing to help you achieve them. It's vital to surround yourself with reputable and supportive people in your career life.

5   Don't Reinvent the Wheel

Rather than using the trial and error method, stick to what is known about success. You must read, study, and try different proven principles that are available to you. Choose to learn something new that applies to your chosen field every single day. Discover how others before you achieved their success, and compare that to what you need to do today to help yourself succeed.

6   Be Unique

Brand yourself as the exclusive business in your target market. Is there something that you know you can do that no one else offers or that you could do it better? What is stopping you from being the best at what you do? If you provide a quality service/product your customers will always be loyal to you.

This doesn't mean you won't have competition in the future, however. Once you start succeeding at what you do, others will be following your example. That's why it's crucial to build alliances early and avoid creating enemies. A good reputation is fundamental to your career.

7 Develop Strategic Thinking Systems

In order to be time-efficient, you must utilize the tools available to you. This may mean systems such as priority planning, to do lists, office hours, or even specific meeting days. Streamline all of your business protocols for maximum productivity. That includes, but is not limited to, your daily, weekly, monthly, and annual duties and responsibilities.

Other examples of such systems include doing some of your important but repetitive work in bulk, finding a new application to use for productivity, or hiring someone to help you with specific tasks. Always be on the lookout for new ways to do things that will help you save time and money.

8 Expand Your Marketing Reach

Diversify your online and offline marketing portfolio. Always be open to trying something new, different and creative, but never stop at a one-time opportunity. It has been my experience that repetitive efforts are rewarded the most.

Some areas that you can expand on include website management, running a blog, article submission, local and internet press release campaigns, venture partnerships, link exchanges, charity sponsorships, public speaking, radio interviews, teleseminars, volunteerism, search engine optimization/marketing, building power networks, and hosting local events.

9   Experiment for a Positive Bottom Line

For every new formula, system, or marketing campaign you try, you must always test and track your results. Stay accountable to your bottom-line or end goal. Be patient enough to see results and persistent enough to gain the most from your efforts.

When something does not turn out the way that you expect, learn to adapt and try something new. It's important that you not expect miracles the first time you try something new. Everything takes time and work; you just have to find the most efficient way for you.

10   Envisioning Goes Beyond Goal Setting

Envisioning your goal means being able to apply all of your senses. You need to know what it will be like to touch, taste, smell, see and hear your goal once you've accomplished it before you can ever start.

The moment that you decide to make a change should become so vivid in your mind that it drives you forward, even when you face obstacles. Your positive focus will fill your workdays with fun, and you will be able to be proud of your efforts rather than disappointed with your unfinished tasks.

Coaching Moment

In this chapter, you learned how to become an empowered woman in the workplace. First, we discussed the opportunities and down-falls women face when asking for a raise or promotion in their field. We also examine one of the most controversial topics in regards to women in the workforce, the wage gap.

Even though women are at a disadvantage and are often undervalued in their careers, we all are capable of learning and mastering new skills – soft skills, which are imperative in the workforce. Do not wait. Research opportunities such as online courses or webinars that offer skills you need to empower yourself in the workplace.

Political Empowerment

"*I raise up my voice – not so I can shout,*
but so that those without a voice can be heard…
we cannot succeed when half of us are held back."

—Malala Yousafzai

Women have made significant progress in many areas from education to health to labor force and even political participation. However, women still face many barriers to their political involvement and representation, both of which are imperative to gender equality and women's rights. Political empowerment is necessary to give women a voice in the policies that affect their lives from pay equality, health care, leadership opportunities and management, to childcare and others. For instance, economic and political empowerment are not mutually exclusive. They are mutually reinforcing.

Women cannot achieve empowerment unless they participate in policies that affect their lives, at home and in the workplace. They need to be politically informed and active, and they need to take power in their hands. Power is not given.

Become Politically Aware

> *"Development without democracy is improbable.*
> *Democracy without women is impossible."*

> —MADELEINE K. ALBRIGHT

To become politically empowered, you must first become politically aware. This means making sure that you seek accurate and relevant information to inform yourself about current governmental policies relevant to you. Knowledge, as we discussed earlier, becomes powerful when we use it to advance a cause or to help us improve our lives. Political participation is not optional or a once every four years voting activity. We cannot affect change that way. We need to empower ourselves and ask for what we deserve. No one will do it for us. We have to stop pretending that everything is fine or that somehow our gender pay inequality will solve on its own, that we will have the right to prenatal care and childcare and that we will have equal leadership opportunities in the workplace. We need to take action to address these inequalities.

Become Politically Active

> *"The people of this country, not special interest big money,*
> *should be the source of all political power."*

> —PAUL WELLSTONE

Active political participation is a way of life. There are different ways to participate and become politically active. Women's business organizations, networking with other women owned businesses, running for local and state level political office, school board, community association, all of these are examples of ways for women to empower themselves. The only thing we cannot afford to do is to become complacent and to hope someone else will do it for us. We owe it to the women before us who fought to have the rights we enjoy today. We owe it to ourselves because we deserve equal opportunity in every area of society. And we owe it to the next generation whose access to equal opportunity and empowerment depends on the actions we take today.

Women in Politics

"There never will be complete equality until women themselves help to make laws and elect lawmakers."

—Susan B. Anthony

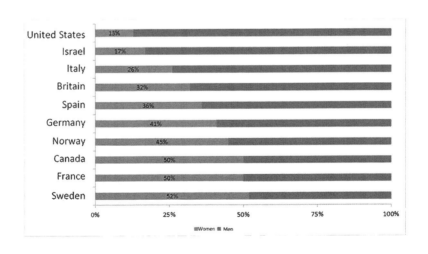

Global Gender Composition of Governments (March 2017)[28]

It is disconcerting to see women's political representation in several democratic countries around the world with the United Stated leading with an abysmal 13% gender equality, the lowest of all. By contrast, Sweden's government consist of a female majority and France and Canada achieved gender equality.

In 2017, in the United States women hold:

✓ 21 percent of seats in the U.S. Senate

✓ 19.1 percent of seats in the U.S. House of Representatives

✓ 24.6 percent of state-level elective offices

Globally:[29] The United States ranks 101 out of 193 countries, with 21 women in the Senate and 84 women in the House of Representatives as indicated above. There are thirty-two female leaders in countries or self-ruling territories.

There are many reasons that women are underrepresented at every level of government. Some of it is due to a lack of participation and interest in getting involved to run for a political office at the local levels. Candidates need financial support to run successful campaigns. A study performed by the Brookings Institute in 2016 shows that "In terms of fundraising and vote totals, the consensus among researchers is the complete absence of overt gender bias"[30] (Why Are Women Still Not Running for Public Office, Brookings Institute., 2016. Web).

Whether we like it or not, it is time to change our political attitude and become informed and active participants in legislative issues that affect our lives. We cannot afford to remain ignorant or pretend that everything is just fine. It is not. Lawmakers, mostly men, are the majority at every level of government, and therefore they will decide what we deserve. They are the majority and therefore have the political power. Women do not. Therefore, men are determining issues related to women's health and well-being.

Exercise – What is Your Political IQ?

Go online to the Pew Research[31] or google "test political IQ" and test your political knowledge. Record your results in your journal.

How did you do? Give yourself a score and take it again until you earn full points or answer each question correctly.

Additionally, find your local and state representatives and call their office to ask questions about issues that matter to you. They work on your behalf taking care of problems that matter to you and your community. They are your public servants.

Last, sign up for your representatives' newsletter to receive updates and stay informed.

Coaching Moment

Women's political empowerment means taking accountability for yourself and your community by being aware, informed, and active. We need to change our attitude toward politics and take our rightful share of power back. We will not achieve gender pay equality or financial empowerment if we continue to get 80 cents for every dollar a man makes or 60 cents and 56 cents respectively for women of color and minority. Political empowerment is imperative to gender equality and opportunity. Therefore, an essential part of becoming an empowered woman requires you to advocate for yourself politically.

The Empowered Woman

"A woman with a voice is, by definition, a strong woman."

—MELINDA GATES

Every woman deserves to be happy and in control of her life. You may wish to focus on one aspect of your life, such as your emotional life, your health, your finances, your career, or political empowerment. At the end of the day, however, you understand that there is no single way to achieve overall happiness and success. As we have discussed in earlier chapters and will cover again here, becoming an empowered woman means being honest with yourself, knowing who you are and what you want out of life. You will no longer rely on others to tell you what to do, what to think and how to spend your time and money.

Too many choices

"Everything in your life is a reflection of a choice you have made. If you want a different result, make a different choice."

—UNKNOWN

We make choices every day. In fact, we sometimes have so many options that we find it hard to choose. However, the simpler our life, the easier it becomes to make the right choice. A woman can only become self-empowered when she realizes that life is a journey, not a destination. When you learn how to tackle your problems head-on and speak up for what you want, you will be able to live the true meaning of life. Moreover, you will feel more confident to know that despite the hard times, you will not lose faith in yourself. Instead, you choose to keep your spirits high rather than getting annoyed or frustrated. Also, you will gradually learn to be grateful for what you have and won't waste time thinking about what you don't have.

In the end, the most limiting obstacles we have in life are the ones we impose upon ourselves. We often buy stuff we don't need with money we do not have to impress people who do not care. Why? We can change this the more aware we become of who we are, what makes us happy and begin accepting ourselves just as we are.

YOU are strong.

YOU are beautiful.

YOU are confident.

YOU are resilient.

YOU are perfect.

YOU are enough.

YOU are in control.

YOU are smart.

YOU are empowered.

Spiritual Awareness

"Beyond my visible nature is my invisible Spirit.
This is the foundation of Life and
I am their beginning and end."

—BHAGAVAD GITA

Self-empowerment and self-awareness reinforce each other. To become a self-empowered woman, you must know who you are, what makes you happy, and what you deserve. Self-empowerment is a connection between your body, soul, and mind. At the base of these concepts, is spiritual awareness. In fact, spiritual awareness is the basis of every other form of empowerment a woman can achieve.

To become spiritually aware, it is first important to understand what it means. Most people associate the term 'spiritual' with religious norms and belief, but that is not necessarily the case. In fact, whether you are associated with religion or not does not determine your level of spirituality. Spiritual awareness is about improving your life by being aware of your feelings and emotions. It is about knowing yourself and being true to yourself. Pretending to be someone you are not or competing with the Jones's, even when it seems that is what society wants us to do is not the way to empowerment and happiness. Resist the urge to let anyone else tell you how to live your life, spend your money, how to dress or how to behave.

Spiritual awareness is about giving importance and time to yourself and spending the time to awaken your consciousness, which is often lost in a busy routine. It is all about knowing yourself and exploring all aspects of yourself to read your soul. It is about knowing your likes and dislikes, your needs, your priorities, your wishes, your goals, the triggers of your happiness and the causes of your pain and miseries. It is about studying the facts of your life to determine what is worth your time and stress and what is not, all the while developing your self-awareness.

Becoming Spiritually Aware

Spiritual growth is the foundation for a better life, one free of fear, anxiety, and negativity. It means becoming aware of the present moment and behaving in harmony. Spiritual awareness comes from within. Make an effort to feel spiritually connected to yourself every day. This may mean taking fifteen or twenty minutes by yourself out in nature to think about your life, desires, needs, and expectations. The deeper connection that spiritual awareness has to your soul, the deeper impact it has on your life and your mind. I begin my day with meditation[32] and do it again several times throughout a day. My life would never have had the clarity and the vision it now has if I had not begun to meditate years ago. I am at peace because I know that I am trying to do the right thing every day.

Ways to Develop Spiritual Growth

1   The only thing that matters is the present. Think of where you are right now, pause for a second and notice how you feel. Try to understand why you feel the way you do. If you recognize and problem and it's something you can control then do something about it. If not, let it go.

2   We create our thoughts. If something negative arises to consciousness, acknowledge it but do understand that you can change it into positive. You have control over your mind so do not give power to negative thoughts.

3   Control your reaction to what happens to you. Anger is poison to your health. We all have bad days or events beyond our control that interfere with our mood. However, by being aware of how we feel, we can control our emotions. After all, we should not spend any time being angry and upset. There is no purpose in that.

4   Suspend judgment. I know it is not easy but it is important to train your mind to accept the world "as is" not as you wish it were. Doing so will allow you to feel liberated and empowered. Most women care what others think of them, and as a result, they sometimes have trouble being happy with themselves. You and I can do better than that. Stop looking for validation from other people, social media or material things. Your value and worth come from within you. Work on yourself and your power within will unleash your potential.

5   Don't conform to everything society tells us we should do. Be authentic and follow your heart. Action speaks louder than words. Act with integrity and you will never have regrets.

6   Being overly comfortable rarely brings us growth. Do not be afraid to take on challenges that push your mind, body, and soul. It is exactly what we need to keep getting stronger, wiser, and happier.

7   Learn to let go. Release any negativity from your body and mind. Do only the things that matter and that make a difference. Don't just be "busy" doing nothing. Live your life with intention and purpose.

8   Smile. Smile as soon as you wake up. Smile at people on the street as you greet them. It is a wonderful feeling.

9   Be grateful. Write down everything you are grateful for, and you will realize that you do have everything you need.

10 Meditate. Stay present. Live YOUR life by YOUR rules.

Exercise

In your journal, record your thoughts every day. When you are honest about your feelings and thoughts, you become aware of your behavior and are more likely to address things that need to change. You may find that your thoughts are often about your personality, the way you look and feel. You are more than that. Becoming aware and at peace with yourself will allow you to control your feelings, acknowledge and release the negative ones and keep the positive one. You will then become in control of your thoughts and feelings and be able to let go of meaningless thoughts.

Coaching Moment

Spiritual awareness is imperative to self-empowerment. Only when you become spiritually aware, do you truly know yourself. You have a better understanding of your desires, values, morals, and thought processes.

Take time out for yourself. Take a walk. Make some tea and read an empowering book. Read this book again, Take action. Get in touch with me. Go to a spiritual retreat with your girlfriends. I guarantee you that you will be back from a self-development retreat or seminar as a "new woman" just as I did after I went on my Bikram yoga retreat for the first time several years ago.

Empowered women create opportunities for themselves to rejuvenate and recharge. Becoming spiritually aware means that you have arrived. You know you deserve to be kind and loving to yourself. No one will love and respect you unless you love and respect yourself first.

Stop Making Excuses

"History has shown us that courage can be contagious and hope can take on a life of its own."

—Michelle Obama

Fear No More

Fear can hinder you from achieving your goals. The antidote to fear is knowledge. If you want something badly enough, there are no limits to what you can achieve. As your knowledge grows, you become more confident and determined to take the necessary course of action to achieve your goals. Fear can sabotage any effort you make towards setting goals.

Develop Confidence

Develop your confidence by educating yourself. Find out what skills you need, and master them. Utilize the advantage the digital age gives you by finding an online course. Go to my website for more resources[33].

Develop your confidence by surrounding yourself with empowered, like-minded women, coaches and mentors. It is important to note that if you surround yourself with confident people who believe in you, you will become more confident. Don't forget that the people around us affect how we feel and think about ourselves. Confidence is contagious.

Develop your confidence by identifying programs and services that will empower you to stand out from your competition and operate in excellence within your niche. Is there a tool or program out there that could help you get a step forward? I am sure there is. You just need to take action now to find out.

Tips to build your confidence now:

1   Take care of your appearance

2   Recognize your insecurities and work on them

3   Keep fit-healthy

4   Wear clothes that compliment your body and skin tone

5   Smile at everyone and say hello

6   Compliment people

7   Do not be afraid of challenges – it is a sign of growth

8   Admit when you are wrong and ask questions

9   Never compare yourself with others

10 Being confident is a journey, not a destination

11 Celebrate your successes and tell everyone about it

12 Tell yourself – "I am amazing", "I am empowered"

Develop Courage

What is courage?

- ✓ Mental or moral strength to resist opposition, danger or hardship

- ✓ Courage implies firmness of mind and a strong will in the face of danger

- ✓ Standing firm in your values and beliefs

- ✓ Speaking up, showing, up, sharing your ideas

Building courage will help you take steps to a brighter future that you ordinarily would not take. When you build courage, you begin to take risks and put fear behind you. Courage is the process of admitting that you have fears, yet you are willing to find a way to defeat them without allowing them to control you.

A woman that has learned to accept responsibility for her own future is a courageous woman. It is vital that we accept the blame and responsibility when we fail and review our actions to learn from our mistakes moving forward. You will not find courageous people stepping back when opportunities come their way; they will always step to the front.

One essential key to building courage is to involve yourself in self-improvement. Learn what new traits you need to succeed, and make a plan to expand your abilities.

Inner peace and feeling content with oneself is also vital to building courage. Someone who is content and has inner peace will behave well under pressure and realize that there are things that happen in life that are beyond our control.

The "I Don't Have Enough Time" Excuse

How often have you heard people say, I do not have enough time? Maybe you have even said it yourself. Well, I am here to tell you that is an excuse.

You will not be surprised to learn that each one of us has the same amount of time – 24 hours in a day – and yet some of us are far more effective in how we manage our time relative to what we need to do.

Multitasking is not effective. It is a myth. It is a waste of time, money and energy. It is impossible to focus on more than one task at a time and do a good job. Think about how many times you have tried to balance your checkbook, write a research paper while on the phone and cooking all at the same time. Most likely, none of the tasks was done well, and you won't remember the conversation you had and the food was overcooked. Not to mention that you lose concentration and mental energy when you try to focus on too many things at once. Stress also accumulates due to multitasking, which will make you feel overwhelmed, irritated and even hungry. Why would you do that to yourself? There is a better way – remember that knowledge is power only when it is acted upon. Otherwise, it is useless.

Developing Your Time Management Skills

Time management requires that you have a clear vision of your goals and the results you want to achieve. Having goals without having a plan to reach them won't do anything for you. It is imperative that you spend some time to study how time management works and then apply it to your own life. You'll never again say that you do not have enough time to get things done. In fact, you will have plenty of time left over for you to enjoy.

Always have a plan and use my formula – MIT = ROT.

The "It's Too Hard" Excuse

This is a common excuse for why women stop short of achieving their dreams. While it is true that it is human nature to do things the easiest way possible, empowered women do not avoid things because they are difficult. On the contrary, they look adversity in the face and decide to conquer it anyway. Remember the growth mindset. We can only grow if we challenge our minds.

It may seem easier just to give up, but what does that mean for all the time you already spent working towards your goal? Quitting only sets you back and makes things more difficult for you in the long run. Don't run away. Instead, stand firm in your ambitions. You CAN do it.

The "I Don't Feel Like It" Excuse

There are a few reasons why you might not "feel like it." You may lack motivation, feel bored, or just simply want to be lazy. It is important to remember that we all have moments where we simply do not feel like doing anything, and that's just fine. Take a break, relax, recharge and then go back and continue your project.

The "It's Not My Fault" Excuse

This excuse can lead to a slippery slope of depression and feel at a loss with oneself. People who use the excuse, "it's not my fault," lack accountability. They do not take responsibility for their own actions and act as though things are not in their control. The biggest problem here is, if you cannot take responsibility for your failures, you will not get the chance to take responsibility for your success.

An empowered woman knows that she will make mistakes along the way, but she is not afraid to own up to them. Instead, she takes the opportunity to learn from her mistakes and applies her new knowledge going forward.

The next time you are about to use this excuse, truly think about your situation and the things you could have done to make the outcome different. If an issue is, in fact, your fault, do not be afraid to admit it. Own your failures, so that, when the time comes, you can own your success.

Coaching Moment

Excuses will not give us success or power. Excuses are for people who are not accountable or responsible. That it is not you.

Fear has no power on its own. It is in our minds. We can overcome it and we discussed several ways of doing that. To resist fear, you must build courage and keep working at your goals no matter what. We do not avoid things because "it's too hard." Empowered women find a way to complete their goals. They are smart, pro-active and resilient and they always push forward.

Plan For Success

"We are what we repeatedly do.
Therefore, excellence is not an act but a habit."

—Aristotle

Practice is key. None of us is perfect, but we can always make progress toward becoming stronger, wiser, kinder and more empowered. If you have made it this far, you know that you deserve to be happy. I hope that you have also decided to stop making excuses. Now that you have decided you want to make changes, you may begin designing your life and your goals around your values. In this chapter, we will go over the importance of choosing happiness, as well as understanding that your past does not determine your future. We will also go over things that you should avoid as well as what you should actively do to keep yourself on track.

We all have to start somewhere and dreaming may be the first step. Growing up in a communist country, all I could do was dream of one day becoming educated, successful and even moving to America and pursuing the American Dream. Sure, back in the 80s that may have sounded like an unrealistic dream but a dream nonetheless. Dreams are about making things happen. Therefore, I made sure I was good in school, learned English and French, which both were mandatory and got involved in activities that would increase my knowledge and confidence. I loved learning English, and with hard work and practice, I felt that I became quite good at it. When I had a chance to leave the country, I felt prepared to use my English skills and integrate into my new country (though I knew I would have to perfect my English when I was able to speak with native English speakers). I knew that people would judge me by the way I communicated and presented myself and I quickly learned that opportunities show up to those who are prepared. My preparation has never stopped. I improve every day because there is no perfection. We learn and grow for as long as we live. That's an amazing thought to be able to live each day knowing that we get better every day.

Choose Happiness

> *"If you are depressed, you are living in the past.*
> *If you are anxious, you are living in the future.*
> *If you are at peace, you are living in the present."*
>
> —LAO TZU

To be happy is a choice. It is a lifelong commitment that we pursue happiness each day by making informed decisions aligned with our values and principles. If you are not happy now and have no plans to change, how do you expect anything different tomorrow? You can choose to keep doing the same things you always have done, or you can choose to make a change. It probably will not be easy, but if it is something that you have a drive for, it will be worth it to you in the end.

My passion is teaching and empowering people to live meaning-ful, purpose-driven lives. My passion is what drives me forward and makes every day worth it. It is time for you to find your passion and pursue it too. Know that you deserve happiness, you just have to find a way and continuously work for it; never give up.

It is unfortunate that so many people are unaware that living "a good life" is within reach, and it begins with a choice. You have the choice to believe that you deserve better and that you will allow nothing or no one to tell you otherwise.

Failure is life telling us that we need to do something differently. The fact that you did not succeed at a task does not mean you cannot do it. Suspend any negative judgment, try new techniques and keep working at it. You might be surprised. Do not forget that failure is part of success. Allow yourself to fail but do not allow yourself to give up. That is too easy and you should regard giving up as not an option.

If you are ready to move forward in your life, choose happiness today.

There is no more time to wait!

Learn How to Work For Productivity

"If you want to change your life, you have to first change the way you think – it's that simple
OR MAYBE NOT."

153

The Pareto Principle[34]

It is time that you learn to use the 80/20 Rule, also known as the "Pareto Principle". Named after its founder, Wilfredo Pareto[35], an Italian economist, who noticed that 80 percent of income in Italy went to 20 percent of the Italian population. There were two categories of people, "the few," or the 20 percent of people who enjoyed money, influence – the people at the top, and "the many," or the 80 percent, who were people at the bottom. Now let's apply the Pareto Principal to your life and find out how it may help you achieve growth and success. When taken personally, the numbers may change. However, the most important thing here to understand is that there are certain activities that you MUST do (your 20%) which account for the majority (your 80%) of your happiness – money, health, relationship and so on. What are they? What are your passions? What are your values?

What do you love to do that makes you happy and possibly wealthy? Review your most important values, and then you will be ready to use and apply the 80/20 rule to your life. Once you do that you will never again say that there is not enough time to accomplish the things that matter to YOU. Remember, not everything is equally important. Therefore, you need to find out your 20% and work at it every day to get the most benefits from it. That is the Pareto Principle briefly.

Example of my 80/20 Life

I learned years ago that to change my life I needed to change my mindset. To improve my life, I needed to learn and apply strategies that would give me the most ROT – return on my time.

Therefore, I began reading, listening, taking courses, attending seminars, and studying successful people's habits and strategies. My new mindset allowed me to believe in my abilities and that I could improve in any area of my life as long as I was committed to doing the work. After all, I had accomplished a few challenging goals and believed I could do anything I set my mind to do. However, that was not enough. Belief alone does not produce results unless we take action to learn the strategies and principles that allow us to maximize our output. The Pareto Principle, allowed me to implement it in my life and get the best results from my efforts.

For instance, I focus on my passions and activities that produce the best results (output). I enjoy teaching and empowering women, so I focused on teaching, interacting, podcasting, creating courses and webinars, Skyping and presenting information that make women's lives better. These activities are my 20% because they produce 80% of my happiness. For instance, I have written this book in the AM hours because that is when I am most creative and productive. I use the 80/20 rule and focus on it first thing in the morning. To get 80% out of my writing effort, I need to eliminate any distractions such as phone, emails, or anything that could potentially slow me down or break my creativity and thinking process. Later in the day when I get tired, or my peak mental and physical condition begins to fade, I change activities and work on something else. I might be working on a project that produces fewer benefits but doesn't require that I focus 100 percent mentally. Such projects are nonetheless important. I use this time to do things such as responding to emails, reading books and learning new ways of doing things, so I further eliminate any waste of my time.

Know That Your Past Does Not Determine Your Future

"You are not your past but to succeed
you need to understand it."

Most parents want a better life for their children, and my parents were no different. They never wanted me to spend my life as a farmer like they did. They had no choice in their own lives but I did. I accepted the responsibility to do whatever I needed to change my life. More importantly, I believed I could change because I was raised by my parents to believe that through effort, hard work and perseverance I could achieve anything I wanted. I learned to embrace failure, and continue towards achieving my goals.

Think about Thomas Edison, whose teachers told him that he was "too stupid to learn anything." Or Albert Einstein, whose speech was delayed and was thought to be mentally handicapped. Or J.K Rowling who, while living on welfare, divorced, and caring for her children, wrote the Harry Potter fantasy series. Or Stephen King, whose first book, Carrie, was rejected 30 times. Last but not least, the legendary basketball player, Michael Jordan, who attributes success to his many failures. What do these people have in common? They never let their failures determine their success. They persisted. They never gave up.

Therefore, you see that these people and so many others have never given up despite the many challenges and failures they had along the way. No one becomes better at anything by hiding their failures or pretending to be someone they are not. Instead, we become our best selves by demanding the best of ourselves, implementing successful habits, challenging our abilities and persisting against all the odds. This is precisely the mindset that we need to develop to ensure success in every area of our life.

Positive Habits of Empowered Women

We all know women in our lives who are confident, resilient against adversity and who always seem to be in control of their lives. How do they do it?

1   They Have a Purpose

Empowered women focus on their strengths, and while they acknowledge their weaknesses, they know that perfection does not exist. Their purpose in life gives them direction and reason to seek opportunities in which they excel. My purpose is to empower women and girls around the world to reach their dreams and to overcome personal and professional challenges. What's yours?

2   They are Confident

One of the main reasons women doubt their abilities is a lack of self-confidence. Confidence is a learned behavior, and you have access to it. It is in your mind. It is normal to have days when you feel less assured. However, you should be careful and not let others influence how you feel about yourself. When we have a bad day, we do not blame others for it. Instead, we take the time to reflect and to learn from the experience.

3   They Don't Try to Please Everyone

Empowered women lead from the heart. They know that their truth is their freedom. They do not need external validation or "likes" to feel good about themselves.

4   They Make Conscious Choices

Empowered women live with purpose and intention. Their choices reflect the life they lead. Their choices are in alignment with their values, which guide their purpose and behavior.

5   They Do Not Take Things Personally

Empowered women are kind and respectful of others' opinions. However, they make their own informed choices whether others like it or not. Someone's opinions of others is usually a reflection of themselves. Therefore, empowered women do not take others' opinions personally.

6   They Are Their Own Advocates

Empowered women are prepared to fight for what they need and believe. They are their own advocates. If we are not speaking up for our rights, who will? If we are not standing up for justice, who will? I am my own advocate as well as for those without a voice. That is why I wrote this book, to empower women everywhere. To empower YOU. Together we are stronger.

7 They Care For Their Health

Empowered women know that a healthy image, a strong mind and body are imperative to living a long, happy and successful life. They do not waste time on social media or other mindless activities. They live with intention every day and know that what they do and say is important. Therefore, they make informed decisions to maximize desired outcomes.

8 They Protect Their Castle

Empowered women live a simple but meaningful life. Their house is free of clutter, full of natural light, and decorated with pieces that symbolize happiness and create positive energy. They know that a happy home environment affects their mood and well-being. If you need help organizing your home to represent the new you – the empowered woman – you may want to look into Feng shui[36] – my personal choice – to learn how to do it or other simple decorating methods that suits your personality. It is so simple and so rewarding that you will immediately see a difference in how you feel.

S.M.A.R.T. Goals[37] – Formula For Achieving Goals

You want success. You want power. You want to be empowered and to do it you must learn how to set attainable smart goals for yourself. To achieve any goals, not matter how big or small, you need a plan. The proper and effective way to set goals is using the S.M.A.R.T. method. It is very effective because it provides structure and guidance and it identifies what you want to accomplish. I have been using S.M.A.R.T. goals formula since the 2000s, and it never fails. It is part of my lifestyle, and you will benefit if it becomes part of yours, too. To review, S.M.A.R.T. goals are:

- ✓ Specific

- ✓ Measurable

- ✓ Achievable

- ✓ Relevant

- ✓ Timely

Specific

Goals must be specific. For instance, "I will run a 5K in six months." It is specific in that I am setting a timeline for myself. A vague goal would be, I want to run a 5K, without a time frame. Next, you need to find out the specific behaviors that will allow you to achieve your goal. How often should you train to achieve the goal? When will you train, what time and for how long? Your answers to these questions will allow you to see if you make progress toward your goal or if you need to reassess your strategy. Stay away from ambiguity. You must define the goal.

Measurable

To run a 5K, you need to be able to measure your progress, think about how great you will feel and look. Visualize yourself running the race and again at the finish line with a medal around your neck. To achieve a goal, you need to measure your progress. You need to know how much progress have you made and how long you have left to go. You need to be realistic with yourself and not sabotage your progress or expectations. If you cannot measure your progress, you cannot attain your goal.

Attainable

One of the biggest mistakes women make while setting goals is that they set ambiguous or unattainable goals. You need to have a realistic goal that you will be able to attain. For instance, if you have just begun running, you may need several months to train before you can run a 5K. Likewise, if you set a goal to become a millionaire by next year, it may not be a realistic goal if you are unemployed or make minimum wages. You will most likely be disappointed if you set unrealistic goals.

Do not set yourself up for failure. Instead, make sure you have all the skills and resources necessary to accomplish your goals. Think ahead and be as detailed as possible. If you are not sure how to plan accordingly, do not worry, I will help you.

Relevant

Is running a 5K relevant to you? If your health is important to you, and I hope it is, then you will most likely train, even when you do not feel like it. Make sure your goal is relevant to you and aligns with your values. Another example is to write a book as I am doing right now. To me, it is relevant to write this book because I want to tell my story and help people like yourself achieve their personal success. Although it takes a lot of hard work, perseverance, and determination, what keeps me going is my passion and commitment to making a difference in people's lives, especially those who doubt themselves that they have what it takes to change their lives and be happy. If that is you, then you are on your way to transforming your life. Just keep on reading and implementing the lessons you will learn in this book. Of course, you can always contact me for further guidance.

Time-Bound

A goal must have a timeline for a sense of urgency. To run a 5K, you need a timeline for it. Whether it will be five or six months, set the deadline to something you know you will have time for. If you believe you can do it and it is realistic, then you will most likely train hard and achieve it. You cannot dream about running a 5K or becoming rich one day without a realistic plan and a timeline for it. For instance, I will run a 5K in six months. Alternatively, I will have achieved an income of $75,000 a year by January 2018.

"Time moves slowly, but passes quickly"

—ALICE WALKER

Example of Goals I Achieved Using the S.M.A.R.T. Goal Formula

Goal – Earn a doctor of educational leadership degree

✓ S.M.A.R.T GOAL

Specific – Completed a doctor of education degree in three years

Measurable – I divided the number of courses per semester; allocated time for study, set mini-goals for submitting the work on time, and ongoing coaching. Adjusted as needed to meet deadlines. Taking care of myself – mind, body, and soul – to ensure I had the fortitude to get it all done.

Attainable – to earn such degree it required incredible effort, but I knew I could do it. Many have done it before me, so I thought why not me? I also had already achieved several other goals, which increased my self-efficacy and confidence. I believed I could do it.

Relevant – I was committed to the goal ever since I was a child. You recall my mother's story of not going to school because she did not have money to buy shoes. It was relevant because I wanted to change my family' legacy and my future, and teach women everywhere how to become empowered and achieve their own goals. Knowledge is power when we learn how to use it.

Time-Bound – My goal to achieve the degree in three years allowed me to plan for it. I created weekly, monthly, and yearly goals, measured my progress consistently, adjusted my strategy along the way and always stayed focused and committed to the goal. I made sure my environment in which I lived allowed me to succeed.

Goal achieved: Earned my doctoral degree in three years. (I used the same methods and earned my master's degree in 1.7 years and bachelor's degree in 4 years).

Goal – Run the New York City Marathon

✓ S.M.A.R.T. GOAL

Specific – run 26.2 miles marathon in 8 months

Measurable – trained for 8 months. Measured my progress each week and month and adjusted accordingly. Changed my eating habits, joined support groups, met other runners who were also training for a race and implemented a holistic lifestyle perspective – positive thinking, positive environment, healthy eating habits, meditation.

Attainable – It was a realistic goal and knew I could do it.

Relevant – I always loved to challenge myself. In fact, training and running a marathon was preparation for life. The skills I learned during the training taught me to be even more courageous and take bigger risks.

Time-Bound – 8 months allowed me to train my body for the challenge and to run it injury free.

Goal achieved – Ran the 2007 New York City Marathon in 4:30 minutes.

Goal – Pay off my credit card debt

✓ S.M.A.R.T. GOAL

✓ Specific – pay off $5000 in 12 months.

✓ Measurable – divided the total amount into 12 equal parts.

✓ Attainable – Yes – I automated all payment and made sure available money was in the account. Worked longer hours for extra income and stopped using credit cards.

✓ Relevant – One of my goals has always been financial freedom. There is no better feeling than to be financially independent.

✓ Time-Bound – 12 months.

Goal achieved – paid off $5000 in 12 months.

You Become What You do Every day
"What you think you become.
What you feel you attract.
What you imagine you create."

—BUDDHA

What you become is the result of what you are doing on a daily basis. Doing the same thing day in and day out and expecting to get different results is what Einstein called insanity. One of the secrets to success and self-empowerment is determined by your daily agenda, which should include MIT – ROT and setting S.M.A.R.T. goals.

Successful people manage their time and energy and spend their free time reading and learning new things, attending conferences and seminars where they meet other like-minded people to network. They manage their time, energy, and health and they are in control of their decisions.

Hard decisions are never easy, but they are crucial to our success. I learned discipline and resilience very early in life working alongside my parents in the field collecting crops or planting tobacco, both of which I despised. I did not know then, but my childhood has prepared me for the real world, and I am grateful to my parents for teaching me real-world survival skills. They taught me that anything is possible with discipline, hard work, determination, awareness, and the appropriate disposition.

Learning how to set goals using S.M.A.R.T formula allows me to achieve anything I set my mind to achieve and you can learn how to do it for yourself.

Exercise

In your journal, write one S.M.A.R.T. Goal that you'd like to achieve using the S.M.A.R.T. goal formula. Read again the SMART goal formula chapter to ensure you set yourself up for success. Share your goal with everyone, including myself, on social media. Good luck and get ready to reach your goal.

Coaching Moment

Your life does not just happen. Whether you recognize it or not, you are the creator of your life. You live by design not my chance. The choices you make every day are yours. You choose how to feel: happy or sad. You choose empowerment by how you present yourself to the world – confident, happy, and successful. Every day you have a new opportunity at life to make better choices. You cannot blame others for your actions. You are responsible for your actions.

The Empowered Woman Manifesto

I make my own rules
I am responsible
I am accountable
I speak my own truth
I am beautiful just as I am
I think for myself
I make informed decisions
I know my happiness depends on me
I challenge myself in every way
I live my life with intention and purpose
I don't rely on others to know my worth
I never give up
I persist
I see my failures as stepping stones to my success
I respect my body and take care of it
I exercise every day and eat nutritious food
I take naps
I am proud of me
I am my best company

I surround myself with smart, happy, healthy, and caring people

I inspire and motivate others to become their best

I am kind and I care for other people

I have choices and do my best to make good ones

I practice patience

I have walked in many different kinds of shoes

I define success, and how I achieve it

I am responsible for my happiness

I live a simple uncluttered life

I owe it to myself to be empowered, so I am

I am committed to helping women become empowered as well

I meditate

I vote

I inspire and motivate

I live an empowered life

Living the Life of Your Dreams

"There is no force equal to a woman determined to rise"

—W.E.B. DUBOIS

What matters in life? If we are honest, we know the answer; the relationships we have with other people and the way we choose to live our lives. Are you surrounding yourself with empowering, compassionate, loving, kind and socially conscious people or do you let negative influences control your life? Do you live your life according to your values? Or are you self-centered, pursuing success, prestige and external validation? Are you pursuing your passion and purpose and helping others find their own purpose in life?

You deserve to have the life of your dreams, and you should be willing to fight for it. Believe in yourself and be confident that your life is your own and to live it as you wish according to your expectations. Give yourself permission to pursue your dreams, desires, and missions. Chose to become empowered in every area of your life to ensure decisions are well informed and result in success and happiness. There are no guarantees in life, and we should become aware and appreciative of what we have, the people we love and the memories we make together.

You are in control of your life and your choices. Do not let the media influence your thoughts and your way of life or let selfish people bother you when they "show off" their latest car or fashion shoes and bags. You are not empowered because of the things you own. You are empowered because you live an authentic life. You live in harmony with your values and your conscious decisions help to empower other people and make the world a better place.

Life is long enough if we live it well. If we love well.

Our choices make us happy or sad.

Our choices help us either move forward or backward.

Do not feel guilty for not making the right choice all the time. No one does, but you do have the choice of how to feel about it. Choose to make a better choice next time.

You are now inspired and motivated to change your life. You believe it is possible. You asked yourself – WHY NOT ME. Start taking action now toward a better future. Are you one of the 80 percent of the people who despise their job? You have a choice to change it. Look for another source of income, change careers, or go back to school to improve your skills set. How about opening your own business. You have a choice. How about getting out of debt? Start taking the steps necessary to get in control of your finances. As we discussed, there is no real freedom until we respect and manage our hard-earned money. Start a workout plan that you have been thinking about. Sure, take action and get started. Whatever it is you want to do, just do it. Take responsibility for your success and happiness. Take action NOW.

Living your life with purpose also means helping others. Our generosity and kindness will spread good energy that will have lasting benefits. Become a cheerleader, a support system for other women, and a role model of someone who has created and lives an empowered life. Someone who is living a life of significance and excellence.

The journey to women's empowerment has no end, and we should always strive to work together and to help each other.

Empowered women empower other women.

We need each other.

We are stronger together than we are apart.

The future is your choice!

WHY NOT YOU? BECOME EMPOWRED TODAY!

About the Author

Dr. Val Margarit is an award-winning educator, entrepreneur, author, international speaker, and community leader. She is the founder and CEO of Val Margarit Consulting Services, a consulting and training organization committed to empowerment, excellence, and achievement.

A committed advocate for global education and women's empowerment, Dr. Margarit gives back to world communities as a teacher, volunteer, and benefactor. She serves on The Professional Women's Network International Advisory Board[38]; volunteers as a mentor for helping women overcome their self-limiting beliefs. She currently serves a two-year term as President of the Homeowners Association; Dr. Margarit also teaches various university classes on education leadership, teacher preparation and serves as a dissertation and capstone adviser. She also facilitates workshops on personal leadership, motivation and success and speaks on topics from education equality to women empowerment and gender equality.

She has been recognized with awards such as teacher of the year, excellence in teaching, professionalism and best speech award. She is committed and passionate about making a difference and helping people achieve their goals through education and personal empowerment.

Val has a doctorate in education with a specialization in educational leadership, an education specialist degree, masters and bachelors in sociology and minor in political science.

Dr. Val Margarit is available for seminars, workshops, keynote addresses and personal coaching and training. For more information, please visit www.valmargarit.com

Contact Information

Website: *www.valmargarit.com*

Email: *val@valmargarit.com*

Twitter: *@valmargarit*

LinkedIn: *Linkedin.com/in/valmargarit*

Resources

Big Brothers Big Sisters, *www.bbbs.org*

National Organization for Women, *www.now.org*

Equal Rights Advocates, *www.equalright.org*

Save the Children, *www.savethechildren.net*

Teaching for a Sustainable Future, *http://www.unesco.org/education/tlsf/ mods/theme_c/mod12.html*

Only a Teacher, *http://www.pbs.org/onlyateacher/timeline.html*

Barriers and Bias: The Status of Women in Leadership, *http://www. aauw.org/research/barriers-and-bias/*

Global Fund for Women, *www.globalfundforwomen.org*

National Association for the Advancement of Color People (NAACP), *www.naacp.org*

Poverty USA, *www.povertyusa.org*

Action for Happiness, *www.actionforhappiness.org*

Random Acts of Kindness Foundation, *www.randomactsofkindness.org*

Empowerment resources *http://www.empowermentresources.com/books/ text_only/page5-to.html*

Empower Girls, *http://www.sheheroes.org/2011/02/10-websites-we-love-that-are-helping-empower-girls/*

Official Guide to Government, *https://www.usa.gov/*

U.S. Department of State, *https://www.state.gov/misc/60289.htm*

U.S. Department of Labor, *https://www.dol.gov/wb/*

U.S. Department of Education, *https://www.ed.gov/*

American Civil Liberties Union, *https://www.aclu.org/*

Notes

1   *http://www.dictionary.com/browse/self-empowered*

2   *https://www.cia.gov/library/publications/the-world-factbook/geos/ ro.html* Facts about Romania.

3   *https://en.wikipedia.org/wiki/Ciocile* Ciocile – Romania. My native country.

4   *https://en.wikipedia.org/wiki/Dallas_(TV_series)_in_popular_culture* Dallas the movie.

5   *Rich Man, Poor Man,* David Greene & Boris Sagal, Universal Television, 1976, Mini-series, DVD.

6   *https://www.girlsguidetopm.com/6-reasons-why-networking-is-important/* Why networking is important.

7   *http://www.dictionary.com/browse/self-concept.* The idea or mental image one has of oneself and one's strengths, weaknesses, status.

8   *http://www.dictionary.com/browse/self-esteem.* A realistic respect for or favorable impression of oneself; self-respect

9   *http://www.apa.org/pi/aids/resources/education/self-efficacy.aspx.* Individual's belief of his or her ability to achieve set goals.

10   *https://www.projectsmart.co.uk/brief-history-of-smart-goals.php.* The SMART acronym first appeared in the November 1981 issue of Management Review by George Doran, Arthur Miller, and James Cunningham. The acronym encourages making goals specific, measurable, attainable, realistic and time-bound.

11   *http://hechingerreport.org/how-often-do-community-college-students-who-get-transfer-get-bachelors-degrees/* College graduation rates.

12   *Rich Habits: The Daily Success Habits of Wealthy Individuals, (Corley, 2005)*

13   *https://ocw.mit.edu/index.htm* MIT free courses.

[14] *https://www.edx.org/school/columbiax* Columbia free courses.

[15] *https://www.inc.com/marcel-schwantes/science-says-92-percent-of-people-dont-achieve-goals-heres-how-the-other-8-perce.html* Only 8% of people achieve their goals.

[16] *Mindset: The New Psychology of Success.* How We Can Learn To Fulfill Our Potential. Carol, S. Dweck, PhD. 2005

[17] *https://www.psychologytoday.com/basics/emotional-intelligence.* E.I is the ability to manage emotions.

[18] *http://www.danielgoleman.info/purchase/. Emotional Intelligence:* Why It Can Matter More Than IQ (1995).

[19] *http://www.amenclinics.com/media/change-your-brain-change-your-body-on-pbs/.* Change Your Brain, Change Your Life, by Dr. Amen.

[20] *https://www.mint.com/.* Manage your finances in one place.

[21] *http://www.statisticbrain.com/gym-membership-statistics/* People continue to pay gym membership due long after they stop using it.

[22] *http://www.today.com/style/women-spend-200k-makeup-lifetime-skinstore-com-survey-t109772* Women spending on beauty supplies.

[23] *https://www.linkedin.com/pulse/80-people-linkedin-dont-enjoy-hate-job-dan-thomas* Majority of people do not enjoy their job.

[24] *https://qz.com/793109/a-mckinsey-and-lean-in-report-on-women-in-the-workplace-study-shows-women-are-still-trailing-men-in-opportunities/* Women and opportunity in the workplace.

[25] *http://www.aauw.org/resource/the-simple-truth-about-the-gender-pay-gap/* Gender pay gap.

[26] *http://theglasshammer.com/2017/01/31/takes-seven-seconds-make-good-first-impression/* How long you need to make a first impression.

[27] *https://en.idi.org.il/articles/14034* women in government

[28] *http://www.ipu.org/wmn-e/classif.htm* – Women in national parliaments, The United States ranks 101 in the world with 21 women in the senate and 84 women in the house of representative.

29 *https://www.brookings.edu/research/why-are-women-still-not-running-for-public-office/* – Reasons why women are not running for public office.

30 *http://www.pewresearch.org/quiz/the-news-iq-quiz/* – test your political IQ

31 *http://marc.ucla.edu/mindful-meditations* – free guided meditation.

32 *www.valmargarit.com/blog* Diverse articles on self-empowerment

33 *https://www.amazon.com/80-20-Principle-Secret-Achieving/dp/1486213421* Learn to achieve more with less

34 *http://www.pareto-chart.com/about-vilfredo-pareto.html* Learn about Pareto's life and how the Pareto Principal was born.

35 *http://www.mydomaine.com/feng-shui-home-tips Declutter your home and let happiness come in.*

36 *http://hrweb.mit.edu/performance-development/goal-setting-developmental-planning/smart-goals* Learn to use SMART goal formula. Achieve more in less time. Work smarter.

37 *http://pwnbooks.com/margarit.htm* – Val Margarit – The Professional Woman Network Advisory Board.

SELF-EMPOWERMENT IS A MINDSET

WHY NOT YOU? How to Become an EMPOWERED Woman is a little book with a BIG message – YOU have the power within yourself to create your own destiny and live your life with intention and meaning. Val Margarit shares her inspirational story of sacrifice, persistence, and determination to succeed against all odds. She empowers you to take action towards a better life and not settle for the way things are … instead, dream big, take chances, speak up and make your own choices and decisions.

By the end of *WHY NOT YOU?*
How to Become an EMPOWERED Woman you will…

- Learn to live your life not by hope, chance or luck … but by design.

- Discover how to overcome your limiting beliefs, become confident and in control of your life.

- Identify your true values and passion and design your life around them.

- Become accountable for everything that happens to you – good and bad.

- Master the key areas toward self-empowerment.

Excerpts from *WHY NOT YOU?*
How to Become an EMPOWERED Woman

"You have a powerful mind. You are entitled to have meaningful work, excellent health, financial independence, and happy relationships. You have untapped talent and extrordinary ability within you and once you believe you do, you will be able to achieve everything you could ever want in life. Once you change your thinking and circumstances, your life will change forever."

"You cannot control or change events or people, but you can change how you react to what happens to you. You always have a choice."